SAGE was founded in 1965 by Sara Miller McCune to support the dissemination of usable knowledge by publishing innovative and high-quality research and teaching content. Today, we publish over 900 journals, including those of more than 400 learned societies, more than 800 new books per year, and a growing range of library products including archives, data, case studies, reports, and video. SAGE remains majority-owned by our founder, and after Sara's lifetime will become owned by a charitable trust that secures our continued independence.

Los Angeles | London | New Delhi | Singapore | Washington DC | Melbourne

ADVANCE PRAISE

'The book is a compelling narrative on the choices people have in the digital world to become entrepreneurs. It not just explains the strategic options but also shows how to attain success in each of the options. It is a befitting book for the digital world.'

Hitesh Motwani,
Chief Marketing Officer, Skillopedia

'The book very well illustrates how any individual could become an affiliate marketer following the step-by-step guide Professor Seema provides here. The main salience of the book is that chapters are organized starting with key essentials and building on ideas in detail. This makes the book easily readable and helps readers achieve these objectives with a very good road map of improving on each level of progression to be a successful Internet marketer.'

Avadhoot Jathar,
Partner, Data Science, Kantar Analytics Practice

'It is another book from Professor Seema which is so current and insightful. It takes you from the why to the how of becoming a master digital entrepreneur. It is a must-have handbook for all who want to take the journey to conquer the world of digital marketing and understand how to leverage it to grow their personal wealth.'

Rahul Sen,
Head of Commercial Payments,
American Express, Singapore and Thailand

'Gig economy is growing exponentially. People today want to explore multiple interests and wish to have multiple sources of revenue. The book is the key to unlock the potential of opening up multiple income streams. It is a must-read for those who want more from life. It is a perfect guide for students, influencers and professionals to understand the new-age digital world. It is insightful yet very lucid and simple to read and implement.'

Dr Dwarika Prasad Uniyal,
Pro-Vice Chancellor and Dean, School of Economics and Finance, Rashtreeya Vidyalaya University

'The strategic insights in the book, coupled with an actionable road map, make this book a must-read for budding entrepreneurs. The book is very relevant in the context of the digital world. It's a new-age book which can open doors of financial freedom for its readers!'

Dr Moutusy Maity,
Professor (Marketing), IIM Lucknow

'Digital marketing is a subject which draws attention of all, but still there is a void to get practical inputs. This book not only explains complex topics with simplicity but also keeps the readers glued through its conversational tone. It throws light on various aspects of this new-age profession and broadens the horizon of readers by bringing in more clarity.'

Dr Ajay S. Singh,
Director (Finance), Punatsangchhu Hydroelectric Project, Bhutan

'The book is a must-read in this age of digitization. It is an eye-opener on myriad ways people can become digital entrepreneurs. It shows them a path to start and grow business.'

Dr Ritu Tripathi,
Assistant Professor, IIM Bangalore

HOW TO RULE THE INTERNET AND MAKE MONEY ON EVERY CLICK

SAGE Response, our business books imprint, celebrates its silver jubilee this year. As we reflect on this transformational journey that began with a single title, we thank everyone who has helped us to produce content that is topical and relevant across a varied audience of aspiring managers, working professionals, practitioners and students. We feel privileged that eminent management and leadership experts, professionals and stalwarts from academia supported and trusted us with their work. Over the years, SAGE Response has built an enviable list of practice-based, reader-friendly books that provide creative strategies to keep pace with the rapidly changing global scenario. As we grow and evolve with the times, it is our endeavour to continue to publish books that offer innovative solutions, approaches and perspectives to the disciplines that we serve.

HOW TO RULE THE INTERNET AND MAKE MONEY ON EVERY

SEEMA GUPTA

Los Angeles | London | New Delhi
Singapore | Washington DC | Melbourne

Copyright © Seema Gupta, 2022

All rights reserved. No part of this book may be reproduced or utilized in any form or by any means, electronic or mechanical, including photocopying, recording or by any information storage or retrieval system, without permission in writing from the publisher.

First published in 2022 by

SAGE Publications India Pvt Ltd
B1/I-1 Mohan Cooperative Industrial Area
Mathura Road, New Delhi 110 044, India
www.sagepub.in

SAGE Publications Inc
2455 Teller Road
Thousand Oaks, California 91320, USA

SAGE Publications Ltd
1 Oliver's Yard, 55 City Road
London EC1Y 1SP, United Kingdom

SAGE Publications Asia-Pacific Pte Ltd
18 Cross Street #10-10/11/12
China Square Central
Singapore 048423

Published by Vivek Mehra for SAGE Publications India Pvt Ltd. Typeset in 11/14pt Bembo by Fidus Design Pvt Ltd, Chandigarh.

Library of Congress Cataloging-in-Publication Data
Names: Gupta, Seema, author.
Title: How to rule the internet and make money on every click / Seema Gupta.
Description: First. | New Delhi ; Thousand Oaks, California : SAGE Publications India Pvt Ltd. 2022.
Identifiers: LCCN 2021061725 | ISBN 9789354793561 (paperback) | ISBN 9789354793615 (epub) | ISBN 9789354793622 (ebook)
Subjects: LCSH: Internet marketing–India. | Internet personalities–India.
Classification: LCC HF5415.1265 .G874 2022 | DDC 658.8/720954–dc23/eng/20220211
LC record available at https://lccn.loc.gov/2021061725

ISBN: 978-93-5479-356-1 (PB)

SAGE Team: Neha Pal, Shipra Pant and Rajinder Kaur

Disclaimer: All images/logos used in this book are for representative purposes only and are solely owned by the respective copyright owners.

This book is dedicated to my kids, Mitali and Aditya, for their love which keeps me going. They allow me to focus on my work by being very supportive.

Thank you for choosing a SAGE product!
If you have any comment, observation or feedback,
I would like to personally hear from you.

Please write to me at **contactceo@sagepub.in**

Vivek Mehra, Managing Director and CEO, SAGE India.

Bulk Sales

SAGE India offers special discounts
for purchase of books in bulk.
We also make available special imprints
and excerpts from our books on demand.

For orders and enquiries, write to us at

Marketing Department
SAGE Publications India Pvt Ltd
B1/I-1, Mohan Cooperative Industrial Area
Mathura Road, Post Bag 7
New Delhi 110044, India

E-mail us at **marketing@sagepub.in**

Subscribe to our mailing list
Write to **marketing@sagepub.in**

This book is also available as an e-book.

CONTENTS

List of Abbreviations ix
Preface xi

Chapter 1. Avenues to Earn Money 1
Chapter 2. Freelancing Your Way to Freedom 5
Chapter 3. Networking as a Freelancer 17
Chapter 4. Affiliate Marketing 29
Chapter 5. Building Blocks for Customer Centricity 37
Chapter 6. Salesmanship in Affiliate Marketing 43
Chapter 7. Product Selection in Affiliate Marketing 59
Chapter 8. Leveraging Affiliate Networks 69
Chapter 9. Learn to Play by SEO Rules 93
Chapter 10. Advanced Practices in Affiliate Marketing 103
Chapter 11. Supplementary Wisdom in Affiliate Marketing 115
Chapter 12. Let's Talk Influencer Marketing 127
Chapter 13. Influencer Types: Which Is Best? 141
Chapter 14. How to Become an Influencer? 151
Chapter 15. How E-commerce Makes Money 171

Chapter 16. Make Money via Selling on Amazon   197

Chapter 17. Make Money with Dropshipping   215

About the Author   233

LIST OF ABBREVIATIONS

ALS	Amyotrophic lateral sclerosis
AMP	Accelerated mobile page
ASCI	Advertising Standards Council of India
BOFU	Bottom of the funnel
COGS	Cost of goods sold
CPA	Cost per acquisition
CPA	Cost per action
CPC	Cost per click
CPI	Cost per install
CPS	Cost per sale
CTA	Call to action
CTR	Click-through rate
DSS	Data Security Standard
EFT	Electronic funds transfer
EGV	Electronic gift voucher
EPC	Earning per click
EPM	Earning per 1,000 impressions
FBA	Fulfillment by Amazon
FTC	Federal Trade Commission
ICMP	Institute of Contemporary Music Performance
IMV	Influencer media value
LSI	Latent semantic indexing

MOFU	Middle of the funnel
NEFT	National Electronic Funds Transfer
OSC	On-site conversions
PCI	Payment Card Industry
PCs	Personal computers
POS	Point of sale
ROI	Return on investment
SEO	Search engine optimization
SPN	Service Provider Network
SSL	Secure Sockets Layer
TOFU	Top of the funnel
UGC	User-generated content

PREFACE

Digital marketing is hot and trending. India has a young population graduating from colleges. They are full of dreams and aspirations and are exploring avenues for building their career.

After COVID-19, businesses have shifted to digital marketing. The demand for digital marketing professionals has increased manifold. Many companies, instead of hiring full-time employees, prefer to hire specialists for short-term projects.

Many people value freedom and want to be entrepreneurs. They are scouting for know-how for starting their agencies and start-ups without the risk associated with a typical start-up.

Some people are experts in specific domains and have a passion for a field, be it cooking, fashion, beauty or fitness. They wish to become influencers.

Realizing the massive demand for a trusted, reliable source of knowledge which can guide people to earn money online, I wrote this book.

I aim to empower people by providing them a well-organized, engaging, comprehensive and actionable book on different ways of earning money online so that they can kick-start the entrepreneurial journey.

I find three main ways to make money online: affiliate marketing, influencer marketing and freelancing. I have exciting experiences in each of them, and in this book, I am sharing the tips which worked for me and mistakes which I made so that you don't make the same mistakes.

The highlight of the book is that it focuses on both strategy and execution. The book sets you on the right path to be a digital entrepreneur and guides you on how to implement it. It has conceptual frameworks and concepts which are strategically important. Simultaneously, it is very applied, as it gives a lot of examples and case studies, making it highly relatable. It keeps you hooked with visual diagrams, screenshots and statistics.

I am confident that with the help of this book, you will start your journey as a digital entrepreneur. With passion, hard work and the right attitude, you will succeed. I wish you lots of love and success in your endeavour.

My heartfelt thanks to the team of research assistants—Ashwin, Pranshu Mahajan, Deepakala R., M. D. Danish, Aishwarya Narayanan and B. Vasudha, who collated information, analysed that and drew inferences from that for inclusion in the book.

I will be happy to answer any queries you may have related to the book. You can reach out to me at seema@profseema.com

CHAPTER 1
AVENUES TO EARN MONEY

Gone are the days when you needed money to earn money! Brands no longer control what information is reaching the audience! The Internet has changed the way people interact, businesses run and the world operates. It has created a new virtual world which has opened the floodgates of opportunities. What is exciting about this world is that it is fair! No matter who you are and what you do, it offers the same freedom to everyone.

The things inevitable for running a business earlier such as renting a place, furnishing it and the cost of maintenance are no longer relevant. A smooth website has replaced all these things, and it costs nothing in comparison. With the Internet, the need of every worker to be in the office has become more of a compulsion than a necessity. Companies have started hiring temporary workers online. Specific platforms are designed for hiring temporary workers with skills, which has given birth to a whole new profession called freelancing.

Freelancers have the freedom of working from their home and enjoy flexibility of timings. With the abundance of information available online, the customer can apply every other approach to make it work.

The rule to success is simple. The content on your website should benefit people in some way. Brands are looking to reach their audience via the Internet. Thus, the era of digital advertisement has begun. People can see ads whenever they visit some web page.

While traditional advertising methods target the masses and are very costly, digital ads target a focused audience and are relatively cheaper, as there are billions of websites on which ads can appear. However, there are a few issues with digital ads. Most of the websites are bombarded with too many irrelevant ads, thus making the whole experience annoying. Due to this, people have started using ad blockers on their browsers. Brands have understood the problems associated with conventional digital marketing and come up with new innovative tactics. Content marketing has been the fittest solution to all digital marketing problems. It focuses on using the content as an ad for the brands. It also tackles the issue of ad blockers.

Rather than promoting the product itself, or displaying ads, brands look for intermediaries to reach their audience. These intermediaries are people with a decent following for the content they embed. They have gained a following, primarily because of the honest and genuine content they present. So there is no way they will promote something which they feel is not fit for their followers. All a brand can do is negotiate with the intermediary to post a genuine review. The era of fake publicity does not exist.

Social media platforms such as Facebook, Instagram, YouTube, Pinterest and Reddit have emerged. What is unique about these platforms is their sophisticated algorithms. All these platforms show you content based on what you like. Gradually, some people have gathered quite a following by sharing interesting content. These people are nothing less than celebrities. They have a powerful influence over their audience. These people are called social media influencers.

What is exciting about being an influencer is that it requires minimum-to-no investment to start the journey. But it does require a sound strategy, along with hard work and consistency. The most common niches on social media are travel, fitness, beauty, electronics, lifestyle and gaming.

On the other hand, e-commerce websites have come up with another attractive strategy to make people use their website. They allow these intermediaries promote any product they want, provided it is sold on their website. The catch is that the intermediaries are paid on a commission basis. It means that the higher the number of people they convince to buy the product, more significant are their earnings. This method is called affiliate marketing. It is quite similar to content marketing, as you have to convince somebody with your content. Affiliate programmes offer an array of options to choose from. Most of these programmes let you choose from electronics, health and fitness, books, toys, jewellery, watches, shoes and a lot more categories.

Freelancing, affiliate marketing and influencer marketing are the go-to options for individuals looking for ways to generate revenue, especially for the long term. There is no denying the fact that there are other ways of making money as well. What is different about these three fields is that they are reliable.

But due to the omnipresence of the Internet, there is intense competition in all the above-mentioned fields. Note that all three of them are excellent means of generating revenue if you execute the strategies flawlessly. So to help you to beat the rivals, we will discuss each one of them in detail in the coming chapters.

CHAPTER 2

FREELANCING YOUR WAY TO FREEDOM

Freelancing is freedom, as it brings you freedom of mobility, freedom of time and freedom of choice. 'Freelancer' is a term commonly used for a person who is self-employed and is not necessarily committed to a particular employer on a long-term basis. 'Freelancer' is another name for an on-demand worker. According to *Forbes*, there are more than 53 million freelancers, just in the USA.[1]

India has more than 15 million freelancers, and it is expected that 50 per cent of the workforce will freelance in future.[2]

There are two types of freelancing roles.

1. **Project-based roles:** Freelancers are hired to work on a particular project. The payment is made at the end of the project.

2. **Contract-based roles:** Freelancers are hired on a contract basis for a particular period where they provide a specific service to the company. The payment is made when the freelancer meets all the requirements mentioned in the contract.

---

[1] https://www.forbes.com/sites/elainepofeldt/2017/10/17/are-we-ready-for-a-workforce-that-is-50-freelance/#594a05123f82 (accessed on 15 May 2020).

[2] https://www.thehindubusinessline.com/economy/with-freelancing-on-the-rise-indias-gig-economy-is-going-strong-report/article10022680.ece (accessed on 16 May 2020).

A study conducted in 2018 reveals why people opt for freelancing. A majority of full-time freelancers (81%) said that they enjoyed being their own boss.

Benefits of freelancing are as follows:

- Work from anywhere
- Choose your own assignments
- Make extra income
- Work as per your schedule
- No need to do office politics
- Pursue your passion
- Be your own boss

Having a flexible schedule is another important reason for choosing freelancing. Let us now examine how much freelancers earn worldwide. According to a survey by PayPal in 2017,

- Around 23 per cent of freelancers earn more than ₹60 lakh annually.
- Thirteen per cent earn ₹10–15 lakh annually.
- Eight per cent earn ₹7.5–10 lakh annually.
- Twenty-three per cent earn ₹2.5–5 lakh annually.
- Eleven per cent earn ₹2.5 lakh or less annually.

Another pertinent question is: How satisfied the freelancers are?. According to websiteplanet.com, freelancers are a happy lot with the following statistics[3]:

- Eight per cent have higher morale.
- Eighty-two per cent have lower stress.
- Sixty-eight per cent experience a better quality of life.

---

[3] https://www.websiteplanet.com/blog/freelance-stats/ (accessed on 16 May 2020).

- Sixty-four per cent feel proud about career and have a good health.

So freelancing seems to be providing the right balance between professional and personal lives, along with a decent income.

We have studied the types of freelancers and the pros of being one of them. We will look at a few things you need to do to be a freelancer.

HAVING A CLEAR GOAL

It is essential to have a clear goal. Without clearly defined and easily measurable goals, you are going to have a tough time being a freelancer. There are specific questions that you need to ask yourself.

- Is freelancing a way of earning a helpful extra income?
- Do you ever see yourself as a full-time freelancer? If yes, then in how many years?
- Are you going to use freelancing to gain experience for an entirely different goal? For example, your main job may be in software, but you may have a passion for design, so you may take up freelance work related to design to explore it as a career option.

CHOOSE YOUR NICHE

Choosing your niche is the most crucial point of a freelancer's journey. You are advised to choose something you are passionate about. As a beginner, choose a broad segment. For example, let us say you choose digital marketing as your niche. Digital marketing has many subdomains such as search engine optimization (SEO), content marketing and social media marketing. You can freelance in any of them.

As you progress, pick something more specific. The old saying 'Jack of all trades, master of none' does not work well in the long run. In freelancing, clients prefer experts over the inexperienced, as they want quality. Naturally, experts charge higher for their services. We can take an example of Python freelancers.

According to a study, the expert freelancers in Python charge $24/per hour more than the other freelancers.[4] Also, there are fewer expert freelancers in Python than among the rest of the freelancers.

IDENTIFY YOUR TARGET AUDIENCE

Once you know what you are offering, it is time to figure out who will need your services. Ask yourself the following questions to get a better picture of your target audience.

- Which businesses will find my services beneficial?
- Can an ideal client afford the services I offer?
- Do I have the necessary skills that my ideal client seeks?

These questions will guide you in upgrading your skills to meet the expectations of your audience. Also, these will help you set prices strategically for your services.

BUILD YOUR PORTFOLIO

It is important to build a portfolio, as it will interact with your potential clients for you. The primary task of your portfolio is to create an excellent first impression, showing your best work and the companies you have worked with in the past. It should adequately demonstrate what you bring to the table. Your freelance portfolio must fulfil the following:

- Present your best work and your specialty.
- Highlight your educational qualifications, skills and relevant accomplishments.
- List your contact information and other social media handles.
- Include testimonials.

---

[4] https://blog.finxter.com/full-time-python-freelancer/ (accessed on 17 May 2020).

If you are beginning as a freelancer, then an appreciation of your skills from your former boss/head will work as well. Also, keep updating your portfolio with your recent developments, testimonials from clients, etc.

BUILD A STRONG NETWORK

It is crucial to build a strong network to get a regular flow of work. Since you are not associated with any company, you need to market yourself as a brand. Having a strong network provides psychological support along with financial benefits. Let us look at why freelancers require a network.

Build a Presence

Building a credible presence is essential for every business. Now that you are a freelancer, people in your industry should know about you and your work. Building a strong reputation for expertise goes a long way in attracting clients.

Get New Clients

Every freelancer wants to increase their client base. According to a research, around 70 per cent of the jobs are not published/advertised.[5] Companies find it easier to float the opportunity in the freelancing communities/groups. So it is essential to have a presence in these groups.

Big Projects

Let us suppose that you are hired as a freelancer content writer to work on a big project. The company needs a developer to design their website. As mentioned above, companies prefer recommendations from freelancers for the job. You recommend a developer in your network. It will strengthen your bond with this friend. Also, they

---

[5] https://www.websiteplanet.com/blog/freelance-stats/ (accessed on 16 May 2020).

may return your favour down the line by recommending you to some client.

Improve Your Skill Sets

As you grow your network, you will find people with different working approaches and styles. This will allow you to practise things that you rarely use. Also, it will broaden your perspective as a freelancer. You can always ask for tips and suggestions from experienced players out there, which makes you look hardworking and passionate.

Gain New Friends

Working as a freelancer can get lonely at times, especially when you are a beginner. Getting enough quality work to make ends meet can be daunting at times. Networking will introduce you to like-minded people, who display the same passion as you. They will guide you through the highs and lows. Also, they will compensate for the lack of human interaction which comes with being a freelancer.

Now that we realize the importance of networking, it is time to study some techniques to grow our network.

Friends, Family and Colleagues

It is the easiest yet most-overlooked method to grow your network. Tell everyone you know about yourself and what you do. You must be thinking of how telling your cousin about your work will ever grow your network. Well, there is a possibility that their corporate friend is looking for a freelancer with your skills. People never recommend something they don't know about. So make sure you describe your profession adequately. Keep in touch with them from time to time.

Networking at Local Events

Grow your network by attending events. Although it sounds terrifying for a beginner, it is important to participate in such activities, especially in the early stages of your career. It will increase your presence among fellow freelancers and local companies as well.

Suppose you are a digital marketing freelancer, try to attend marketing events. You can also use these opportunities to bond with the heads of these local companies. It enhances the probability of receiving some work.

Use Social Media

Social media offers a massive platform to gain followers. Use social media to showcase your talent/skill. There are various platforms such as Facebook, LinkedIn and Instagram. Choose the platform which is in harmony with your niche. For example, a photographer will gain from being on Instagram, while a marketer can use LinkedIn.

As you progress, you can increase your presence on more platforms. LinkedIn is a dominant platform to attain clients. Companies often post job offers on LinkedIn. Also, it can be used to connect with your potential client.

RISING NICHES IN FREELANCING

As digital presence is becoming more and more critical, the following are some of the rising niches in freelancing.

Content Writing

The primary job of a content writer is to write content for the Web. It can include e-books, sales copies, podcasts, articles and text for websites. Content writing is a vast field in itself. The great thing about content writing is you do not need to be an expert in the niche to write about it. It is relatively easy to gain decent knowledge about a domain in a few days, which opens up unlimited topics to write about. The following are some of the popular sub-domains in content writing.

- **Long-form/SEO content:** It includes writing articles and posts with 2,000+ words. The content needs to be SEO-friendly to rank higher on Google results.

- **Email sequence/sales funnel:** Email is still a great source of income for many businesses. Writing the sales copy for the funnel is a specialized job.
- **E-books writing:** E-books are gaining popularity among businesses. It is an excellent way for firms to grow their email subscribers' list.

Guest Blogging

Guest blogging involves writing your content on another company's site. It is quite beneficial for freelancers at all levels of the profession. Irrespective of the field, it is essential to write for blogs related to your niche. The benefits of guest blogging are as follows:

- Attract traffic from that blog (where you are guest blogging) to your website. Increase brand awareness and authenticity.
- Build relationships with like-minded individuals.
- Boost your website's authority by getting external links from high-authority domains.

Guest blogging is a great way to expand your audience base. It is a two-way street. On the one hand, guest bloggers get an opportunity to display their work to a new audience. On the other hand, featuring guest posts on the blog provides fresh content from a different perspective to the audience.

How does one start guest blogging?

There are many options, but it is essential to research the nature of the blog before selecting it. Focus on finding posts which align with your niche and your industry. For example, a health-related post on a tech-savvy blog is going to hurt both the parties involved. Here are a few questions that you need to ask before approaching the blog.

- Does the blog have a decent following which interacts through comments or any other way?
- Does the blog's content have a high SEO ranking which would increase your content's ranking?

- Does the blog's content complement your niche?
- Do they have a presence on social media where they will share their content regularly?

A great way of finding blogs and websites to guest post is to search for them on Google. Just find relevant keywords and add 'Write for us' or 'Guest post'. Below are a few examples:

- Healthy eating write for us
- Healthy eating guest post guidelines
- Healthy eating guest posts
- Healthy eating seeking guest posts
- Healthy eating guest post submissions

As every blog has a different set of rules regarding posts, it is necessary to read the rules thoroughly. There may be strict rules on what type of links you can include, who you can mention in your post, etc.

Create a Pitch

After you find the right blog, pitch your content. Every blog demands different things. You need to figure out their needs and come up with at least a bunch of topics.

To get an idea about what they are interested in, look at how long their posts are, their popular high-sharing topics, their popular headlines, etc. It will help you stand out in your pitch.

Once you get selected, you need to write the post. Keep in mind all the guidelines and write your post accordingly.

Do not make the mistake of pitching the same idea to multiple blogs. If you pitch your idea to 10 blogs, and more than 1 select your pitch, you are in trouble! Then you cannot send it to both of them, neither can you change it (as you have mentioned the topic in the pitch).

Even if you want to send out similar topics, try moulding it. For example,

1. Why is S20 the best phone ever?
2. S20 has revolutionized the mobile tech industry.
3. Ten features which make S20 the best phone ever!

Add Your Author Bio

Now comes the reward! The author's biography is the place to market your freelancing profession. A good biography depicts what you are offering, what type of content you write, how people can reach you and about your personality.

We will talk about SEO tips and how to improve the SEO ranking of your content in the later chapters.

Writing guest posts will further your career as a freelancer. As you gain experience, you can create your blog, which will act as your freelancing portfolio.

WEB DEVELOPMENT/DESIGNING

While the primary job in web development is of creating a functioning website, the job of a designer is to design the aesthetics of a website, its user experience and user interface.

If you want to kick-start your career as a web developer (freelancer), you have to be proficient in one of the programming languages. Some of the popular languages for web development are PSS, Python, JAVA, Swift and Ruby. A few popular languages in web designing are HTML or Dynamic HTML, JAVA script and CSS.

The idea is to be familiar with some of these languages and be proficient in one of them. As both the fields are quite similar, freelancers are expected to be skilled in both of them.

Your portfolio website needs to be your best work. Having great testimonials for your web development skills on a lagging website looks suspicious. While freelancers enjoy the liberty to design their websites the way they want, it is important to include the following in your portfolio:

1. It must express your working style like the languages you like to work on, tools you use, etc.
2. Explain how your skills can make your client's life easier. Rather than saying that you design terrific websites, say things like you can help in doubling the traffic to their website.
3. Provide them a way to connect with you. Prompt them to drop you a message.
4. Mention what kind of projects you like to work on. For example, if you want to work on developing a website for small businesses, say so.
5. Add testimonials.
6. Add a free resource.

FREE RESOURCE

As a freelancer, it is wise to find multiple ways to attract people. It can be an e-book or free tips. Provide useful information to them. Giving away some of your work exhibits goodwill and the fact that relationships matter to you more than money. It gives visitors a taste of your signature style and, most importantly, builds your reputation as an expert.

DIGITAL MARKETING

Digital marketing is the use of the Internet, mobile devices, social media, search engines and other channels to reach consumers.

It is a new profession which has risen in the last decade. As a freelancer, it is essential to understand SEO, email marketing and social media marketing. We will cover them in detail in subsequent chapters when we discuss the professions of affiliate marketing and influencer marketing.

CHAPTER 3
NETWORKING AS A FREELANCER

In the previous chapter, we learned about different types of freelancers, the pros of being a freelancer and how to become one. In this chapter, we will look at ways to grow the network, as it is one of the major means of getting work. So let us get started!

Well, let us look at what freelancers think are the top modes of finding work!

As seen in Figure 3.1, a lot of freelancers find work from online marketplaces. Examples of such marketplaces would be the following[1]:

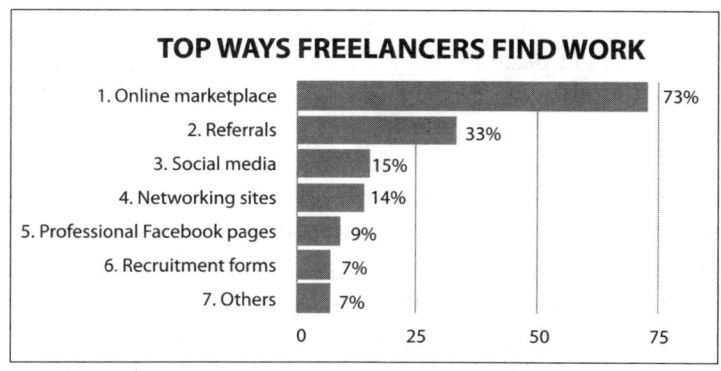

Figure 3.1: Top Sources of Work

Source: https://www.websiteplanet.com/blog/freelance-stats/ (accessed on 25 May 2020).

---

[1] https://anavarre.net/reverse-engineer-freelancing-platforms-to-find-talent/ (accessed on 25 May 2020).

- Fiverr
- Upwork
- QuiGig
- PeoplePerHour
- Freelancer
- Truelancer
- Guru
- WorknHire
- Toptal

All of these provide great opportunities to begin as a freelancer. It is simple to join any of them. These sites will ensure you get plenty of work.

FIVERR

Fiverr is one of the famous names in freelancing websites. Freelancers are supposed to offer their gig, mentioning all the details, and wait for the client to select it. Since it provides gigs for as low as $5, freelancers do not often land high-paying projects. However, Indian freelancers do get the opportunity to earn foreign currency. It is an excellent place for beginners to gain some experience.

UPWORK

Upwork is also a great place to get some work. Unlike Fiverr, the client posts job requirements on the Upwork website, and freelancers apply for it. The platform takes a 10 per cent commission from each side when the client selects someone from the entries received. It is considered a good option for experienced freelancers, as the clients on Upwork are willing to pay more for specialized and quality work.

FREELANCER

What is different about Freelancer.com is that it allows you to compete with other freelancers in contests. The more battles you win, the better is your rating. The fee for fixed-price projects is 10 per cent of the total service price or ₹250, whichever is greater, and 10 per cent of the total service price for hourly projects. However, for a retainer service, if you are subsequently hired, a 20 per cent fee of the total service price is charged.

TOPTAL

This site is meant for developers, designers and financial experts only. They position themselves as the 'website where clients go to hire the top 3% of freelancers'. They do not post writing jobs.

99DESIGNS

This platform is specifically meant for freelance designers. It lets you compete in design contests and get feedback as clients choose the best designers. It is an excellent way for designers to prove their talent.

PEOPLEPERHOUR

It is a great platform, focusing on freelancing for web projects. If you are a designer, web developer, SEO specialist, etc., PeoplePerHour is worth checking out.

DEMAND MEDIA

Demand Media is a platform for the creative types, including writers, filmmakers, producers, photographers and more. You work with the site to create unique content, engage audiences and promote your talent.

As you progress, focus will shift from marketplaces to your social media platforms and referrals for getting work. Experienced freelancers rely on their network to get better-quality work and get paid more.

So let us look at ways to grow your network using social media sites. The most used social media channels are Facebook and LinkedIn. We will discuss a few of them in detail.

FACEBOOK

Freelancers use Facebook groups to connect with like-minded individuals and target businesses as well. But it is a challenging task to find the right group. As of 2019, Facebook had more than 400 million Facebook groups. The sole purpose of joining a group is to create a solid impression and to expand your network along with constant learning. To fully leverage any group, you need to be pretty active and understanding. Naturally, it will consume much of your time. So join a group only if you have the time for it. Full-time freelancers choose three–five groups in which they can actively participate.

How to find the right Facebook group?

With so many options available, there are some groups which you need to avoid, like spam and promotional groups. These groups are used to promote products day in day out, and there is minimal discussion.

First, find the keywords which define your profession. The keyword should be clear and accurate like 'fashion photography' or 'Instagram marketing'. Now search these keywords on Facebook. You will find a lot of groups matching the keyword. Facebook also shows the average number of posts shared every day to give you an idea of how active the group is. Note that all groups are not public. So read the description of the group to check if it matches your preference. If you want to join it, click 'ask to join' and wait for consent.

You can also search the keywords on Google by appending 'Facebook groups' after it (refer to Figure 3.2). Google will show you great articles where people have handpicked the best groups for you.

There are two ways that Facebook groups can benefit you as a freelancer.

Connect with Other Freelancers

The benefit is not only to connect with like-minded individuals but also to help each other grow. As you progress, the more experienced members of the group may help you get a client.

> **The 7 Best Facebook Groups for Inbound Marketers – Impact**
> https://www.impactbnd.com > blog > best-facebook-groups-... ▼
> Mar 8, 2019 - **Social Media** Managers **Group**; CXL - Conversion Optimization, Analytics & Growth; Digital **Marketing** Questions; Women in MarTech; **Marketing** ...
>
> **10 Best Facebook Groups For Online Marketing and Social ...**
> https://www.brianmanon.com > 10-best-facebook-groups-on.... ▼
> Top 10 **Groups** on **Facebook** for Bloggers and Marketers. Here ist a list of the top 10 **Facebook Groups** for **Social Media Marketing**, Bloggers and Entrepreneurs.
>
> **Facebook Groups for Marketing| Brand24 Blog**
> htttps://brand24.com > blog > grow-your-business-with-face... ▼
> Content Marketing| **Social Media Marketing**. 6 Clever Ways to Use **Facebook Groups** for Growing Your Business. How many **Facebook Groups** do you belong to...
>
> **20 Awesome Marketing Groups on Facebook (to Skyrocket ...**
> https://robertkatai.com > facebook-marketing-groups ▼
> Jul 15, 2019 - 20 **Marketing Groups** on **Facebook** (to Skyrocket Your Skills), less than 1. **Social Media** July 15, 2019 ...

Figure 3.2: Screenshot Grabbed from Google Search for Facebook Groups

They might have a lead which is not a good fit for them but could suit you. As mentioned in the last chapter, you can also make some great friends who guide you professionally and personally.

Connect with Potential Clients

You can also use Facebook groups to connect with your target audience directly (refer to Figure 3.3). Let us suppose you are a bridal makeup artist. You can join 'brides to be' groups.

If you work as a marketer, you can join groups of small businesses near your area.

After joining the group, the first and foremost thing to do is to read the rules of the groups before taking part in any conversation. Once you are familiar with the rules, start conversations by asking

Figure 3.3: Screenshot Grabbed Online for Facebook Groups for Small Businesses

relevant questions or by trying to resolve doubts of other members. The most crucial point is to keep showing up regularly with new inputs. Remember that it is a two-way communication.

Never post the link to your site unless you are asked. Always be respectful to other members. Also, do not spam the group just for finding new ways to promote your stuff. Instead, keep the best interest of the groups at heart. If group members respect you, they will automatically be interested in your work.

Note that these groups are beneficial only if you are regularly involved in them. So set aside some time specifically to network in such groups.

LINKEDIN

LinkedIn always focuses on the user's professional profile unlike other platforms. While 95 per cent of the recruiters use LinkedIn to find ideal job candidates, it is a great place for freelancers to find work.[2]

---

[2] https://anavarre.net/reverse-engineer-freelancing-platforms-to-find-talent/ (accessed on 25 May 2020).

Complete Profile

The first thing to do after joining LinkedIn is to put a face to your name and add a profile picture (refer to figure 3.4). Make sure it is professional, as it accounts for the first impression people will get from your page. As per LinkedIn, members with a profile picture get up to 12× profile views than those without one. The next task is to add a headline. The headline is what appears right below your name.

The headline will be the first thing that visitors to your profile read. It has a limit of 120 words and is a lot like a billboard advertisement for you and what you do. Make it catchy and appealing. Do add the rest of the things such as your experience and skills. Having a complete profile on LinkedIn is crucial.

Show Your Work Sample

While there is nothing wrong with dropping the link to your portfolio website (as mentioned in the previous chapter), you can showcase your work sample on LinkedIn as well, as this makes your work more easily accessible.

Figure 3.4: LinkedIn Profile

Endorsements

People can rate your skill sets on LinkedIn. Also, the higher the number of ratings, the more credible you look, which increases the chances of getting some quality work.

Post Invaluable Content

The best way to create a network is to attract people through your content. Focus your content on topics which matter to them. Posts like '5 Python skills that you need to know' are likely to attract like-minded developers, while posts like 'how to build MVP (minimum value proposition) for your start-up with no programming knowledge' will attract start-ups and small businesses. So plan your content accordingly.

Empathetic

Be empathetic to the people. Help them whenever you can. Remain in touch with your past clients in the network. Ask them about what they are doing and update them about your new skills and projects. Show them that you care. Empathy goes a long way in building a real connection. If your past client requires a freelancer in the future, they will approach you.

Search

You can use the search option in multiple ways.

SEARCH FOR TARGET AUDIENCE

Connect with your ideal client's LinkedIn profile. But you do not want to message them directly. The trick is to look for topics which fascinate them. Start by writing content on these topics to capture their attention.

SEARCH FOR PEOPLE LOOKING FOR YOU

People post on LinkedIn something like 'Looking for a marketer' or 'Know about some Instagram influencer?' to find somebody

Figure 3.5: LinkedIn Search Using Content Filter

for the job (refer to Figure 3.5). You can filter out such posts and directly message them saying that you noticed they were searching for a freelancer. The only problem is that you can search for profiles and businesses, but you have to search among posts and content shared by other members.

So select the 'content' tab before searching.

Always keep in mind that your primary aim to join LinkedIn is to form a real connection and not to sell your product. So avoid jumping directly to the selling phase. Adopt a helping attitude.

Also, you need to be consistent with your content. Engage with your target clients by liking and commenting on their posts.

More, the Merrier

With the changing needs of the market, freelancers feel that having more than a single skill is necessary to survive in a highly competitive environment. According to data from Website Planet, only 5 per cent freelancers rely on one skill. About 61 per cent of the freelancers feel the need to have two–three skills. Around 34 per cent depend on more than three skills. However, as mentioned in the previous chapter, it is necessary to develop expertise in one of them. For example, you can be an expert in content writing along with decent programming skills. Also, freelancers need to keep updating their skill sets to keep up with the competition. Around 70 per cent of full-time freelancers have taken part in some form of skill training within the last six months.[3]

---

[3] https://www.websiteplanet.com/blog/freelance-stats/ (accessed on 26 May 2020).

Laws

Your work belongs to you. Freelancers should always keep in mind that they have copyright over all their creations. The client is paying you for using it. Only you can decide how it can be used or recreated unless you have signed a contract stating otherwise. Since you have the copyright, you can also use your previous work for another project, as long as you do not have an agreement prohibiting any transfer of the right of such work.

According to PayPal, 61 per cent of freelancers in India reported that they were not paid at least once in their career. So it is advised to sign a formal contract before diving into the project to avoid such an experience. A deal must mention the following details:

- Names of both the parties, along with their addresses
- What kind of work will be done by you, how much of it and how the client can use it, and also all the tasks expected from the client and you
- Schedule of payment: When will the payment be made, the mode of payment, the basis of payment, that is, on an hourly or work basis and, if some other way, then how, and how additional charges for extra work will be paid to avoid disputes
- Deadlines: Duration and deadline of the work
- Termination: A clause indicating why and when the agreement will be terminated; all the possible situations should be mentioned to avoid any dispute
- Confidentiality: A clause declaring that your work would not be disclosed to any third party by the client.
- Dispute judgement: A clause must state which course of action should be taken in case of an argument, arbitration, negotiation or court case; however, consult a lawyer in case a dispute arises

PART-TIME FREELANCERS

If you are working for a company and want to start freelancing, you need to be a little careful. Some jobs do not allow you to work parallelly; and if your company finds out, you can lose your job.

Apart from that, part-time freelancers have a hard time figuring out when to pursue freelancing full time and let go of their job. Leaving your primary job too soon leaves you with unnecessary pressure to make ends meet. It is observed that when you can regularly earn 70 per cent of your primary job's income for a few months, then you can officially pursue your freelancing career full time.

Now that you are thorough with the process of being a freelancer, we will talk about affiliate marketing in the next chapter.

CHAPTER 4

AFFILIATE MARKETING

Affiliate marketing has made businesses millions and ordinary people millionaires.

—Bo Bennett, President,
Archieboy Holdings, LLC

The affiliate marketing industry is set to grow up to $6.8 billion, proving how big an industry it is.[1] As the Internet became widely available to the masses, the rise of affiliate marketing was inevitable. Fifteen per cent of the total digital media advertising revenue comes from affiliate marketing. Around 81 per cent of marketers leverage the potential of affiliate marketing. And about 15–30 per cent of all sales for advertisers come through affiliate marketing.[2] The flourishing affiliate marketing industry thus offers us a plethora of opportunities to make money as well as serve the target audience.

What makes the prospects of affiliate marketing even more exciting is the emergence of 3D printers. As technology advances, 3D printers will be a common sight in no time. It will bring drastic changes for businesses, especially e-commerce. One of the major expenses of running a business is the storage of inventory. With

---

[1] https://www.the-reseller-network.com/content/95/what-is-an-affiliate-merchant/ (accessed on 2 December 2019).

[2] https://99firms.com/blog/affiliate-marketing-statistics/#gref (accessed on 2 December 2019).

the rise of 3D printers, businesses will prefer creating products on demand. E-commerce giants like Amazon will soon open many 3D centres, which will reduce delivery time and costs.

With the faster delivery system and reduced cost of the product, e-commerce sites will witness higher order volume, which will benefit the affiliate marketers as well. As more people purchase products through e-commerce sites, your target audience will continue to grow.

WHAT IS AFFILIATE MARKETING?

Affiliate marketing is a form of digital marketing, wherein you persuade someone to buy a product online, and if they buy on your counsel, you receive a commission. As simple as that! For example, if you are promoting a laptop brand online by dropping an affiliate link, then you will earn a stipulated commission for purchases that every user makes through your link. Anyone can become an affiliate marketer by signing up for various affiliate programmes.

HOW DOES AFFILIATE MARKETING WORK?

To understand how affiliate marketing works, refer to the following infographic (Figure 4.1).

Now, let us examine the players in the ecosystem.

Merchant: The Product Owner

A merchant is the party that manufactures the product. In other words, a merchant is a seller or a brand. It can be a big company, like Apple, which produces electronic goods, or even a small enterprise. If you have a product to sell, then you are a merchant too.

For example, if you are working towards the sales of a laptop made by company 'X' through an affiliate network 'Y', then for every sale made by your recommendation, X pays you a commission. Some affiliate merchants (like Amazon) may run their affiliate programmes

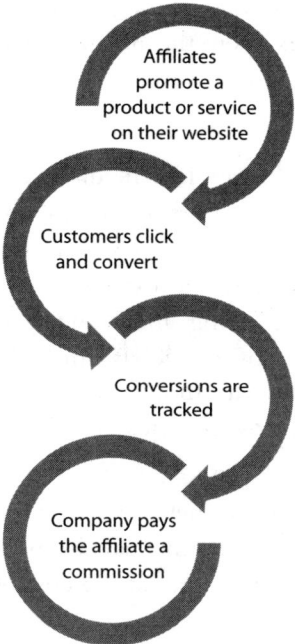

Figure 4.1: Simplified Working of Affiliate Marketing

as they save money in membership fees and commissions payable to affiliate networks. Contemporary examples include Apple, Flipkart, Boat (headphones), etc.

Other technology companies have their affiliate programmes too. You just need to go through their website to get an idea of the same.

Publisher: The Affiliate

The affiliate marketer is also known as the publisher. They are individuals who earn commissions for referring sales through their affiliate link. The mode of advertising is up to the discretion of the publisher. Blog posts, videos and social media are some of the familiar places where the publisher tries to influence customers to buy the product through their link.

Now, the question is how to begin the journey of an affiliate marketer! The answer lies in the affiliate network.

Network

An affiliate network is an intermediary between the merchant and the publisher. It is more than just an intermediary, for it provides benefits to merchants as well as affiliates. It provides ad tracking technology and an expansive database of publishers to merchants, and tracking links and payment processing to the publisher. Some of the ways through which the affiliate network helps affiliates earn money are through cost per sale (CPS), cost per install (CPI), cost per click (CPC) and cost per acquisition (CPA).

A few examples of affiliate networks are Clickbooth, ClickDealer and vCommission. ClickBank has been around for the past 17 years, thus making them one of the credible platforms.

Customer

Well, everyone's a customer! You and I are customers. Customers are the individuals who see, analyse and then decide whether to purchase the product or not. The affiliate will try to market the product to the customer on whatever channel the affiliate deems fit, whether that is through the social network, YouTube videos or a search engine using content marketing on a blog. As soon as the customer clicks the affiliate link, the tracking system works in the background, wherein the customer can follow the purchase process just as usual, and the affiliate still ends up being paid a commission.

AFFILIATE PROGRAMMES

To facilitate a better understanding of affiliate marketing, you can sign up for popular affiliate programmes. Some of them are Amazon affiliate programme, Flipkart Affiliate Program, vCommission and eBay affiliate programme. Getting started with these affiliate programmes is not a challenging task. Just log in to the respective websites and sign up for the plans for free.

Getting Started with Affiliate Marketing

Let us explore the various steps to become an affiliate marketer.

STEP 1

First things first, you have to sign up for an affiliate programme. If you are a beginner, then plans with a vast consumer base are suggested.

STEP 2

As you sign up, an affiliate link tailored explicitly for your username about a particular product will be given to you (we will explore in detail about affiliate link in the next chapter).

STEP 3

You have to publicize the product digitally through various platforms. Websites and blogs are preferred. In case you are an individual, then blog posts with the affiliate link at the bottom would suffice to entice the reader to click on the link.

In many cases, the merchant sites themselves provide flash banner ads and click ads to facilitate the same. You need to feature them on the platform you are comfortable with to publicize. For example, LinkedIn, Instagram, Facebook and Blogspot are some of the familiar platforms that affiliates have been utilizing.

How To Be an Efficient Affiliate Marketer

In the last section, we have seen an overview of how you can get started with affiliate marketing. You might have observed that setting yourself as an affiliate marketer is simple. But the challenging part is how you can flourish efficiently. The steps to achieve efficiency are given below.

STEP 1

Find the most profitable industry. This can vary with the trends online; so keeping yourself updated is essential if you want to grow in the marketing field. A larger audience ensures that you get a minimum flow of profit, but experienced affiliate marketers prefer to cater to a specific audience. Given below are some of the most popular industries for affiliate marketing.

- **Beauty:** To give you an idea, the worldwide cosmetics industry is worth $170 billion.[3]
- **Health and wellness:** With the health and wellness industry on the verge of hitting $1 trillion, it is one of the most preferred niches among affiliates. Market Health, Global Healing Center, Buddha Groove and many more offer lucrative health affiliate programmes.
- **Expensive hobbies:** When it comes to expensive hobbies, the first thing that strikes our mind is golf. And there are quite several golf affiliate programmes as well. If promoted efficiently, this niche can roll out significant profits.
- **Outdoor survival:** Who does not want to stimulate some adrenaline? Well, everyone does, and that is the main reason this point is on our list. Survivallife.com run by Ryan Deiss and digitalmarketer.com are survivalist blogs aimed at promoting products for survival like mountaineering gears, etc.

STEP 2

After finding a suitable industry which matches the current trends, you have to pick a niche for your videos or the blog itself. Niche essentially means the domain in which you have a prowess. For example, electronics can be your industry, and smartphones can be

---

[3] https://www.affilorama.com/blog/beauty-blog-101 (accessed on 7 December 2019).

your niche. You need to present your recommendation with utmost clarity in such a way that even a layperson visiting your blog/video can connect to what you wish to convey. So choose a niche which makes you feel like an expert.

STEP 3

Now, the essential part involves choosing a product to promote. In the case of smartphones, there are a lot of brands in the market. You have to choose which product to promote based on two criteria. One, you can select them based on their brand value and market capitalization. Two, you can choose them based on your personal preferences as well. In the first case, the consumer already has a mind map about the phone. So you just need to develop engaging content to ensure the visitor clicks on your affiliate link. However, in the second case, the effort to persuade the consumers to your way of thinking plays a vital role in pushing them towards clicking the link and reaching the merchant site. In Figure 4.2, we see a YouTube channel named Tamil Talkies promoting a stock broking

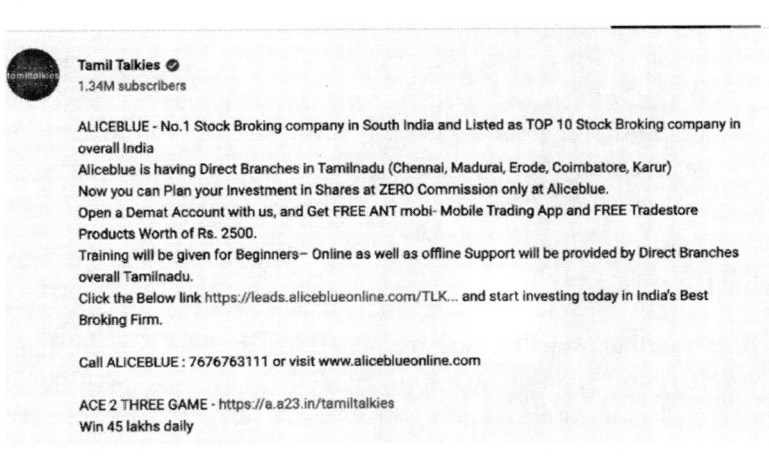

Figure 4.2: Screenshot Showing Tailor-made Affiliate Links in the Comment Section

Source: https://www.youtube.com/c/TamilTalkies (accessed on 7 January 2020).

company by the name Alice Blue and an online game by the word Ace 2 Three Game (see description in the image). If you observe the affiliate links, you can find that it is tailor-made for Tamil Talkies.

Following all the above steps, you can generate good traffic towards your merchant site, thereby increasing the probability of converting those clicks into sales.

CHAPTER 5

BUILDING BLOCKS FOR CUSTOMER CENTRICITY

Affiliate marketing is an excellent opportunity if you truly believe in the value of the product you're selling. In the last chapter, we got an understanding of what affiliate marketing is and how it works.

In this chapter, we will analyse how you must have a customer-centric approach to build your affiliate marketing business.

There are a lot of affiliate marketers online. The thumb rule is to prioritize the customers. In affiliate marketing, not everyone is immensely successful.

This happens because marketers prioritize profits over the customer. Publicizing products without having enough knowledge about them can cause a slump in profits. To prevent profits from declining, you must recommend only those products in which you have a niche and a first-hand experience. Your content will then sound convincing and radiate confidence, which will push the customer to take the leap of faith and buy. Figure 5.1 gives us an idea about some of the most profitable niches.

The practice of prioritizing the customers by promoting products that you feel will genuinely help your audience can work wonders in the long run. Winning customers' trust and retaining it over time will roll out profits for you. To be successful as an affiliate marketer, you must adopt the following thumb rules.

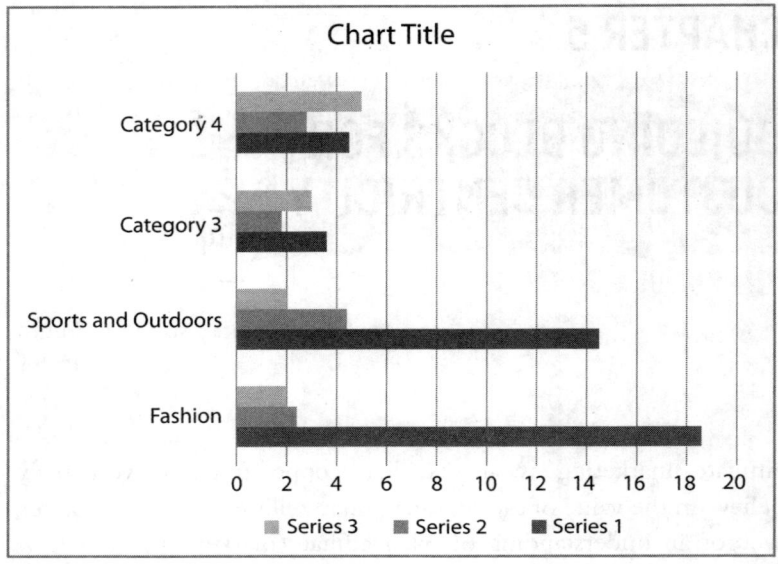

Figure 5.1: Popular Affiliate Categories

Source: https://www.amnavigator.com/blog/2015/09/25/analysis-of-best-affiliate-programs-top-20-niches/ (accessed on 26 October 2020).

MAKE CUSTOMERS FOR LIFE

In the previous section, we have talked about the 'trust factor'. For the continued trust, you have to build a strong rapport with your audience, as this eventually turns them into subscribers from just being transient customers. With this practice, you would know what exactly your customer needs and cater to the same. In this way, the connect increases, and thereby you can identify more relevant products which satisfy the needs of your 'fan base'. So an important question arises as to how one can start building a strong relationship with a customer.

It is simple! Identify a target audience which shares a common snag or a common objective. Once you have figured out the audience, you can put forth your solutions and ideas through affiliate marketing. Through this effort, you are essentially influencing a bunch of like-minded people to buy products through your recommendation, which will solve their problems and fulfil their objectives as well. Just remember that a genuine two-way relationship takes time to build. You must show patience as well as make the efforts to build a healthy relationship. Although the whole process is time-consuming, it is definitely worth the wait! So here are a few tips to speed up the entire process.

ANNOUNCE YOUR PRESENCE

You have to open up your personality and interests. This might sound absurd to you, but the more the customer knows about you, the higher will be the chances they will read your post. In simple words, a sense of attachment develops when people relate with the person on the other side of the screen. So remember to divulge your personality apart from being a marketer.

ENGAGE WITH THE AUDIENCE

The first step is to urge your audience to give comments about your content or clarify any doubt they have. Remember that leaving your audience's comments unattended make you look rude. So make sure you reply to the comments. Encourage them to take out some time to post a review. You will get to know not only what it is about your content that your audience likes or dislikes but also about the problems they are facing.

Consider using the Google Keyword Planner tool to check the monthly search volume of a product/service which you wish to promote. Following this technique would allow you to choose products or categories which have high search volume.

Another critical question is: What is the ideal number of products that you must promote to become an established affiliate marketer? Well, it depends on the individual, but the following pie chart (Figure 5.2) shows the number of products that affiliates prefer to promote.

Looking at the pie chart, it is evident that affiliates usually prefer to promote 1–10 products (42.17%), followed by 11–20 products.

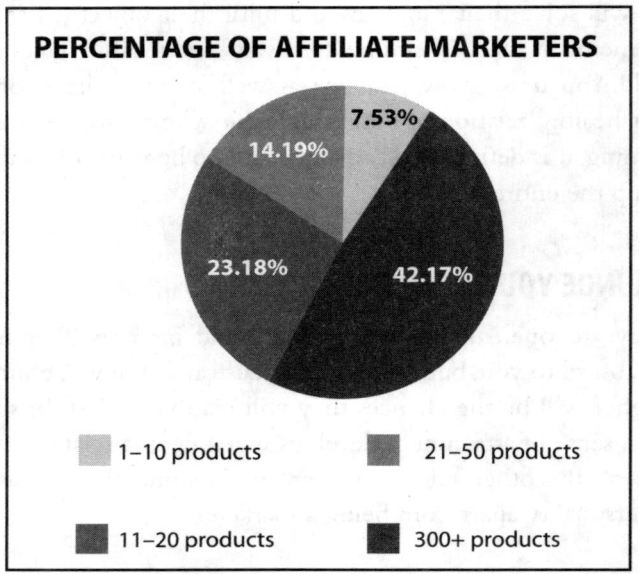

Figure 5.2: Preference of Affiliates for the Number of Products
Source: https://99firms.com/blog/affiliate-marketing-statistics/#gref (accessed on 26 October 2020).

Just make sure you never compromise on the quality of your content.

EXPERIENCE SPEAKS A LOT

Sharing your own experience is the best way to publicize the product, as you are letting the visitors know how it feels to use the product. It is analogous to see the review of an app in Google Play Store before downloading it. A study has proven that around 72 per cent of consumers trust online reviews as much as personal recommendations, thereby proving to us how vital it is to share product experience to push sales.[1]

---

[1] https://www.yotpo.com/blog/word-of-mouth-marketing/ (accessed on 3 December 2019).

One of the standard practices to establish product experiences is live unboxing, especially in the category of smartphones. There are more than 20 million search results.[2]

As large as 68 per cent of the customers trust the experience of other consumers about the same product.[3] So a genuine review gives the audience an idea about the pros and cons, thereby allowing them to make a thoughtful decision on the purchase of the product. Just keep in mind that your primary goal as an affiliate marketer is to help your audience make a better decision. This, in the long run, builds the trust factor as well. So in simple words, experience pays off.

---

[2] https://www.efomi.com/unboxing-can-increase-sales-e-commerce/ (accessed on 3 December 2019).

[3] https://www.yotpo.com/blog/word-of-mouth-marketing/ (accessed on 3 December 2019).

CHAPTER 6

SALESMANSHIP IN AFFILIATE MARKETING

In the last chapter, we discussed the importance of customer centricity in affiliate marketing. In this chapter, we will discuss how to sell effectively.

The most challenging part of affiliate marketing is selling the product through your link. Some of the most effective sales techniques are landing pages, email campaigns, social media messaging, blog posts and YouTube videos. Let us explore each method one by one.

LANDING PAGES

The landing page is a standalone web page, created with a specific purpose of marketing or running an advertising campaign. It is where a visitor 'lands' after clicking on an image in an email or ads from Google, YouTube, Facebook, Instagram or similar social media sites. According to estimates, companies with 30 or more landing pages generate 7 times more leads than those with less than 10.[1] A landing page is different from the website, as the objective of the landing page is conversion. It has no navigation, has minimal distraction and reinforces buy buttons.

It's pretty much unadorned and directly flashes a single button to take up the course. This simplicity in landing pages is why we expect a high conversion rate once the visitor clicks on the post.

---

[1] https://www.slideshare.net/iFactoryDigital/30-amazing-landing-page-statistics (accessed on 12 April 2019).

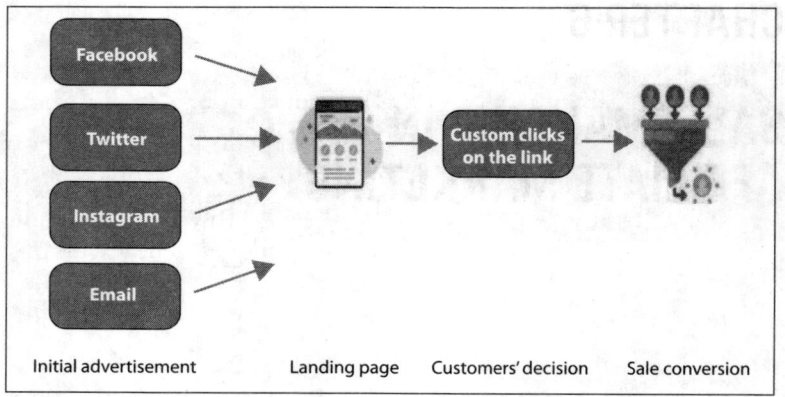

Figure 6.1: Flow Chart Showing the Functioning of a Typical Landing Page

The landing pages have an intense focus on the objective of the marketing campaign, and this focus is what we refer to as the call to action (CTA). Figure 6.1 provides a quick and intuitive understanding of the essence of the landing page.

EMAIL PLATFORM FOR MARKETING CAMPAIGNS

Email campaigning is the oldest and one of the most effective means to generate CTA, considering its massive user base. A study by the Radicati Group estimates that by 2022, there will be around 4.2 billion email users.[2] This is an enormous chunk of current active Internet users, and if correctly leveraged, it can do wonders for you as an affiliate marketer. You could run email marketing campaigns as an affiliate marketer on products which you feel could cater to the needs of your subscribed email database. It is not just sending links but understanding the role of a healthy relationship, as mentioned in the previous chapter. When an affiliate shares a link in

---

[2] https://www.radicati.com/wp/wpcontent/uploads/2018/01/Email_Statistics_Report 2018-2022_Executive_Summary.pdf (accessed on 12 April 2019).

the form of a mailer, the moment you click on the image, it takes you to the merchant site, asking you to take action.

There are tools to conduct auto follow-ups through emails. Some of them are GMass, Mailchimp, Zoho Campaigns and Mixmax. Utilizing these tools, you can optimize your time. Amazon's affiliate programme doesn't allow you to use affiliate links directly in emails. I will tell you about some smart techniques to deal with this problem in the later chapters.

SOCIAL MEDIA MESSAGING

In this section, let us concentrate on affiliate marketing on the LinkedIn platform. LinkedIn visitors have been on the rise, as the platform encompasses a wide range of features, more than being just a social media network, such as jobs and work. If you are a beginner, you can use LinkedIn messaging as a useful tool to promote your products. A message can be sent to a LinkedIn user. As the user scrolls down, they find a CTA button; clicking on it would lead the user to a landing page or merchant site. Purchasing the product or not is up to the visitor's discretion, but increasing the focus through messaging a user exclusively is what affects the conversion rate positively.

Let us now examine affiliate marketing on Instagram. Affiliate links on Instagram are perhaps the most ideal approaches to inactively bring in cash on the stage. There are many ways you can add affiliate links to Instagram. However, only a few of them provide you with significant income. Your Instagram bio is by far the most promising location to add affiliate links. As people visit your profile page, they will likely be interested in reading more about you. This will enable them to understand you better. While doing so, they will surely land on the affiliate links. Curious to see what you are promoting, they will end up clicking on the link and land on the company's website. If you are getting your commission based on the number of clicks you achieve, then this will earn you a lot of money. The only prerequisite for this to work is that you must be active on Instagram and have many followers.

BLOGS: THE MOST PREFERRED MEDIUM OF SHARING AFFILIATE LINKS

Blog posts are the primary platform for promoting products. You can follow some tested and straightforward practices to get the most out of it.

Be Genuine in Blog Post

Well, it is mandatory to disclose to your audience that you are using affiliate links in your content and that you will earn a commission, at no expense of their own, if they make a purchase using the link. This is primarily because scams in the past have hit the affiliate marketing industry pretty hard, thereby influencing the people to shrug away from clicking on the link. This makes you look honest and authentic, thus building the trust. Also, some people are oblivious to affiliate links, so they directly open a new web page of the merchant site and make purchases. So you are losing out on commission. To ensure this does not happen, you have to announce yourself as an affiliate, earn the readers' trust and sincerely drop the links.

A simple act of helping out a customer who's perplexed about one of the products you have promoted can script a long-lasting impact on their mind. So, as discussed in the last chapter, encourage your audience to put forward their doubts in the comments, and make sure you respond to each of them. By this practice, you show how interactive you are, and your motto is not just to earn a commission but also to serve the audience.

Drop Links Multiple Times; It Doesn't Cost Anything

Generally, a blog post can get a bit longer as the marketer is keen on giving the nuances of the product with all the technicalities and comparisons. Often, the question arises as to where exactly one has to drop the link to gain maximum clicks, which affects the rate of conversion. Well, there is no 'single position' where you can achieve that. To explain why it is not the case of a single position, consider a reader who scrolls through your blog, which has the affiliate link at the beginning of the post. He scrolls down the post and eventually forgets to click on the affiliate link—and you have lost a potential commission. You might face a similar scenario when you drop your link at last, as some readers might not scroll through the entire blog post. To avoid such an outcome, affiliates drop links multiple times where they feel any average reader would be enticed to make a purchase decision. It can be at the beginning and end or somewhere in the middle of the blog post.

YOUTUBE: THE GO-TO PLATFORM

The number of monthly active users on YouTube is 2 billion, with around 30 million daily active YouTube users as of 2019, which means that 95 per cent of the global Internet population watches YouTube.[3] How big is that for a consumer base! There are thousands of videos uploaded every day, which attract millions of views. All these factors have made YouTube a go-to platform for affiliate marketing.

Offer Them More Than What They Want

Offering users more can come in many forms, including a simple bonus coupon or a referral code which can further qualify them to avail discount over the product. Since a lot of YouTubers are already following this technique, you, as an affiliate marketer, have to give them perks which are more relevant to the product you promote. The following pie chart (Figure 6.2) provides us with an idea about what customers generally prefer.

An obvious observation from the pie chart is that customers are more likely to prefer products which come with discounts or are

---
[3] https://www.omnicoreagency.com/youtube-statistics/ (accessed on 12 April 2019).

Figure 6.2: Customer's Preference for Benefits Offered

Source: https://i.pinimg.com/474x/7c/be/80/7cbe801611a46b6c7f65af7618
8bfbec--loyalty-dog.jpg (accessed on 12 April 2019).

free. This is why experienced affiliate marketers are more inclined towards offering more than just what the consumer needs.

Let us consider an example of a YouTuber who solely reviews products. This is important to the field of affiliate marketing, as the YouTuber shares their hands-on experience of the product. And in the course of the video, they recommend the viewers to check out the link in the description.

To share your content on YouTube, you will need the following props.

1. **Decent-quality camera:** A friendly smartphone camera can also work, but the quality of the video needs to be professional. Anything less than 480 pixels isn't good enough.

2. **Microphone:** If people are going to listen, you need to make sure that your voice is clear. For that, you need to buy a microphone of decent quality.

3. **Studio-like set-up:** You won't need a proper studio in the beginning, but try to look for an excellent place to shoot. The site must look appealing and professional, and make sure the location is quiet.

4. **Script:** Prepare yourself a script which covers everything you are going to convey, especially when you are a beginner. As you get more used to speaking in front of the camera, you can use a presentation instead of a script.

5. **Tripod:** Use a tripod to handle the camera so that there is no shaking.

6. **Video editing software:** It is incredibly essential for YouTube. As a beginner, you can use free software like Windows Movie Maker, which provides vital functions. If you want more features, you can opt for a premium product like Sony Vegas or Adobe Premiere.

7. **Decent processor:** Video editing software takes a lot of your computer's RAM. So make sure your computer has a decent processor which can use these video editing software easily.

8. **Hard drive:** Raw video footages can easily use hundreds of GB of your computer storage; so it is advised to get yourself a 2–3 TB hard drive (saving such huge files on the cloud can be costly).

Now, certain things will help you with your YouTube journey.

1. **Consistency:** You need to upload high-quality content on your channel consistently. YouTubers also mention the schedule of their next video; for example, Jeff Nippard (gym and workout videos) posts only on Tuesdays. Even if people like your content, they will land on your YouTube profile page and check out more content. No one subscribes to a channel for a single video. So make sure you have uploaded an ample number of videos.

2. **Catchy title:** Imagine that your typical target viewers go through YouTube and your video flashes on their screen. Apart

from factors such as the number of likes and views (which are not in your control), you have one major factor in your hand which will influence if users are going to watch the video—a catchy headline. Your video title must sound interesting and convey the central message of your video in some way, for example, 'Phone XX is Great. Don't Buy It'.

3. **Thumbnail:** A catchy thumbnail can entice the users to click and view the video. The thumbnail of your video must clearly define what the video contains. If your thumbnail promises something different, then people will bounce off your video, thus decreasing your rating in the YouTube algorithm. Various industries prefer different aesthetics in the thumbnail. While the gaming industry opts for bright thumbnails which convey an 'awesome' factor, the education industry chooses simple and elegant thumbnails which make them look professional.

4. **High audience retention:** Since the amount of content on YouTube is unbelievable, making your viewers watch your video till the end is a difficult task. YouTube's algorithm favours watch time and channels which can hold viewers for longer. Also, if your viewers don't watch it till the end, they aren't going to subscribe to your channel.

- Apart from thumbnail and title, you need to avoid monotony in your voice and must sound energetic and excited about your content.

- Also, make things like your introduction and like and subscribe request as short as possible.

- One important thing is that your content must be valuable to your audience, and you must not keep rambling on the same points.

- Engage with your audience through comments, likes and encourage them to drop their opinion. 'YouTube's algorithm favours videos with more likes and comments.

- YouTube also offers the option of polling question which you can use to know more about your audience's opinion.
- And last but not least, please stick to your niche. Inconsistency in the type of content a YouTuber posts is generally not appreciated.

5. **Description:** YouTube uses video description to understand the concept of your video. It strongly recommends that you optimize your video description for better SEO ranking. So here are some practices which will aid you in writing great descriptions.

Write long and thorough descriptions (at least more than 200 words). Your video description is as important as your content. So take time to write an excellent description.

Focus more on the first two–three sentences. YouTube's algorithm puts way more weight on the first two–three sentences of your description. YouTube recommends you to use primary keywords early in the description. To get the people to click on your video, start your description by explaining how the video will benefit the viewers. Do not make the mistake of providing your social media details early in the description.

Apart from getting your video a higher ranking in search results, using essential keywords increases the chances of getting more clicks. Since the first few sentences show up in the search results, people tend to select videos with more matching keywords in their description.

- Make sure you repeat the primary keywords at least two–three times. Also, try to use some supplementary keywords; for example, if your content focuses on how to become an entrepreneur, then focus on keywords such as 'passive 'income' and ''start-up' (Figure 6.3).
- Do not use the same video description for different videos. Every piece of content must have its own description.
- Also, make your video description conversational and energetic.

Figure 6.4 shows a template that you can use for preparing the video description.

1) FREELANCER:
If you have a hobby like Web designing, content writing, then freelancing can be beneficial for you. Just join a site like Freelancer.com and select your niche.
Also, create a good portfolio. Mention the previous projects that you have worked on.

2) BLOGGING
If you are passionate about something, for example, smartphones, books, etc., then you can start a blog. Once you can attract a decent amount of traffic to your website, You can earn from multiple sources like ads, affiliate marketing, promotion.
Google AdSense
Google AdSense is one of the ways to make money. if your blog drives a decent amount of traffic, Google will pay you for putting up ads on it.

3) AFFILIATE MARKETING
If you have a blog Affiliate marketing is a genuine way of making money. There are lots of companies with affiliate program like Amazon, Flipkart, etc.
All you need to do is promote a product, and every time someone buys using your link, you get a commission. These programs are free to join.

4) CONSULTANT
The first step of being a consultant is to have the skill. People consult an expert for their opinion. So you need to be an expert. Well, it's not as challenging as it sounds.

5) EARNING MONEY FROM FIVERR
Fiverr is an excellent place to make money online, especially if you are a student because it helps you in getting work.

Figure 6.3: Using Secondary Keywords

Source: www.youtube.com/c/profseemagupta (accessed on 15 January 2020).

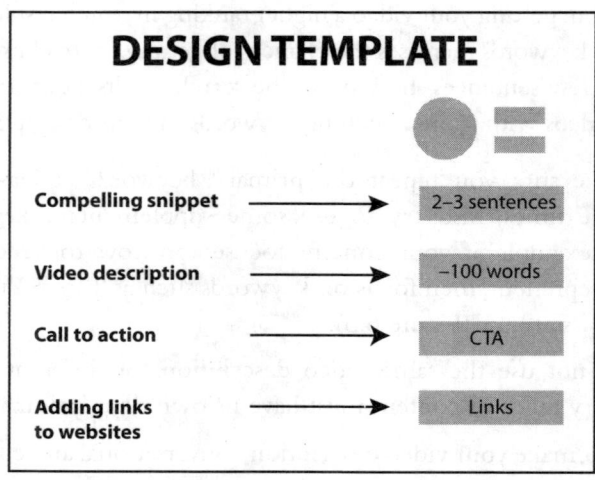

Figure 6.4: Template for Video Description

- Optimize your description for suggested videos. YouTube states that the video's metadata (and the entire description) plays a vital role in the suggested video algorithm. The trick is to understand the videos for which your content can be suggested. No matter how good your content on football is, it will never be suggested after the viewer watches a photoshop video.
- So check for your competition videos. Search your primary keyword on YouTube and read the description of the top three–four videos (apart from your video). Figure out the relevant keywords in those videos and incorporate them in your video description.

Figure 6.5 summarizes the different factors which contribute to the ranking of your video.

It is exciting to watch the first category: 'enjoy what I like' mindset. This is the USP of social media platforms such as YouTube and

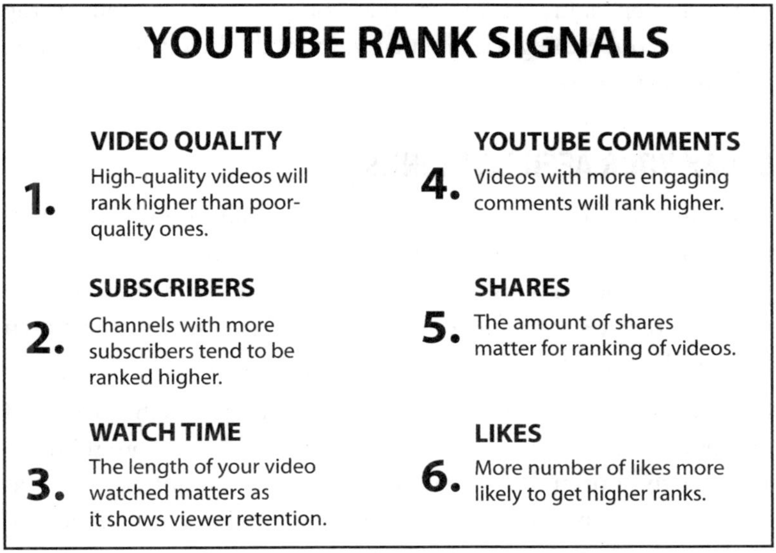

YOUTUBE RANK SIGNALS

1. VIDEO QUALITY
High-quality videos will rank higher than poor-quality ones.

2. SUBSCRIBERS
Channels with more subscribers tend to be ranked higher.

3. WATCH TIME
The length of your video watched matters as it shows viewer retention.

4. YOUTUBE COMMENTS
Videos with more engaging comments will rank higher.

5. SHARES
The amount of shares matter for ranking of videos.

6. LIKES
More number of likes more likely to get higher ranks.

Figure 6.5: Factors Contributing to the Ranking of the Video

Instagram. People will randomly scroll through these sites to find something interesting, which they don't usually do on Google search.

The first category is so frictionless that people with no interest or prior knowledge of the content can be drawn to watch it. This increases every video's audience base to potentially everybody.

Some videos, such as a video of test fire of machine guns, have a whopping 28 million views.[4]

Many of the viewers may be interested in the video because they might never see someone use a machine gun in real life. But was that something they wholeheartedly desired?

Well, for some of them, yes! But the others were mostly bored and were looking for something interesting. We watch over 1 billion hours of YouTube videos a day, more than Netflix and Facebook videos combined. Everyone out there using YouTube to avoid boredom is a potential viewer of your content.

Now, it doesn't mean that you leave your niche and get a gun to gain some followers. It just means that you will never fall short of the audience. Just make sure that you post your content in the rest of the three categories regularly; soon, the benefits of the first category will follow.

CLOAK YOUR AFFILIATE LINKS

The idea of cloaking was introduced to avoid commission theft through malware software that gets loaded unsuspectingly on people's computers. This malware observes the pages those people visit and replace the affiliate links on those pages, with their own affiliate ID code, thereby stealing their commission.

Link cloaking is a perfect way to fight these thefts. It is the process of disguising your affiliate links (provided by the affiliate programme) into much shorter links that the computer cannot interpret as affiliate links. The link will show the address of some section of your website, but clicking on it will take you to the affiliate site.

---

[4] https://www.youtube.com/watch?v=bmeRROzi_4k (accessed on 7 December 2021).

There are various benefits of cloaking your links, other than theft protection.

1. **Trust:** People are always a bit reluctant to click on affiliate links. However, cloaking your links increases your click-through rate (CTR). Additionally, by cloaking your affiliate link, you can decide what the URL looks like. So instead of a link to a product page on some other site with random numbers and product IDs which make no sense to your audience, you can change the URL to match whatever you like. Rather than showing your visitors a link like http://www.geeky.com/productb23-56, which says nothing about what's on the other side, you can show a URL like example.com/go/sleeping-bag, which quickly tells that the other side contains a sleeping bag.

2. **Management:** As an affiliate, you are going to manage hundreds of affiliate links on your site. The task of handling these affiliate links can get too time-consuming. If you have a WordPress site, you can use a plug-in 'Thirsty Affiliates', as it allows you to organize your affiliate links into categories to keep them in logical groups. All your hosting links will be in a 'hosting' group and all your clothing links in the 'clothing' group. Additionally, it makes the task of inserting affiliate links into blog posts much easier.

3. **Tracking:** You can also track the traffic from your affiliate links, which can provide invaluable insights about which links are getting more attention and then revise your priorities accordingly.

How to Use Thirsty Affiliates

First, you need to download the 'Thirsty Affiliates' plug-in. Search for it in your WordPress dashboard under plug-ins → Add new. It is quite straightforward to use this plug-in. Just remember that the destination URL will be the affiliate link provided by your affiliate programme.

With this plug-in, changing the destination URL of a link is easier than ever, even if you have used it in several places. To change the destination of a cloaked link, you only need to edit the link in 'Thirsty Affiliates' and not all of the posts you have inserted it into.

HOW TO INSERT AFFILIATE LINKS IN VIDEOS

You can insert affiliate links in the description of the YouTube video. During the video, you can direct the attention of the users to the link in the description. The links shared in the video description need not be cloaked. However, you can make them look shorter and prettier by using a URL shortener like Bitly.

As shown in Figure 6.6, you can also use the 'info cards' and 'end screen' features of YouTube to direct the users to your website. Since these features allow you to provide a link to only your website or websites approved by Google, you cannot give affiliate links. Some affiliate marketers use these features to drive traffic to their website, which has affiliate links. From the YouTube studio, you can add these two features to your video while uploading.

Figure 6.6: Info Cards and End Screen

Source: https://www.youtube.com/watch?v=e6G1dRqf7IA&t=1s (accessed on 18 February 2022).

Cards are the notifications that appear on your screen while watching a video. They serve as a tool to drive traffic towards your channel, videos, blog or website and can even be used for polls.

You can add a maximum of five cards per video, but I suggest not overusing them, to create a viewer-friendly experience.

Following are the steps to add cards to your video:

- Click on your channel icon at the top right of your YouTube page.
- Select 'Creator Studio' and then click on 'Video Manager'.
- Click on the video to which you need to add cards. Click the dropdown arrow, and then choose cards.
- Click on the add card and select the kind of card you want to use.
- Format your card as desired, place it where you want it to appear and you're good to go.

End screens can be added within the last 5–20 seconds of your video. They serve as an essential tool to increase your watch time by directing your audience to another video, website, playlist or channel. It will encourage your viewer to explore all aspects of your channel or website.

HOW TO ADD ASSOCIATED WEBSITE TO YOUR CHANNEL

Sign in to YouTube and go to 'Creator Studio'. There, you can add your website and complete the verification process. It will help if your website is added to Google Search Console. After that, go to the 'Settings' tab and then 'Advanced Settings' tab under Channel (Figure 6.7).

After that, click on 'Advanced Channel Settings' and add your website as an associated website. Then, verify, and your website will get connected to your YouTube channel (Figure 6.8).

Figure 6.7: Linking Website to Your Channel

Source: www.youtube.com/c/profseemagupta (accessed on 15 January 2020).

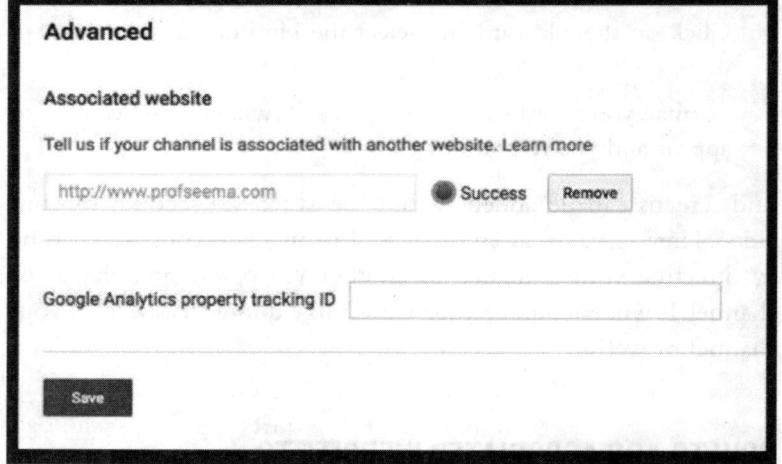

Figure 6.8: Verifying the Website

Source: www.youtube.com/c/profseemagupta (accessed on 15 January 2020).

CHAPTER 7
PRODUCT SELECTION IN AFFILIATE MARKETING

In this chapter, we will examine how to find a niche and its impact on the profits made by an affiliate marketer.

WHAT IS AN AFFILIATE NICHE?

An affiliate niche is a product or service in a category that you promote. It can be anything ranging from a smartphone to a baby soap. Sounds simple? Well, actually not. Choosing a profitable niche is a decisive factor in making profits. Figure 7.1 indicates the percentage of Amazon affiliate accounts in different niches. The Amazon affiliate programme offers you the most extensive consumer base for any product. But the diagram shows that the majority of the affiliates earn from lifestyle products followed by food. A simple explanation of the observed trend is the psychology of humans. Every one of us is striving hard towards leading a better lifestyle. It may be through buying healthcare products, subscribing to fitness services or just festooning our living room with an antique ceramic. The goal of almost every individual on the planet is to lead a better lifestyle than yesterday.

HOW TO FIND A SUITABLE NICHE?

We all know that there are millions of products being sold across the globe. This makes choosing a niche an even more difficult job. The thumb rule of selecting a niche is to see how passionate

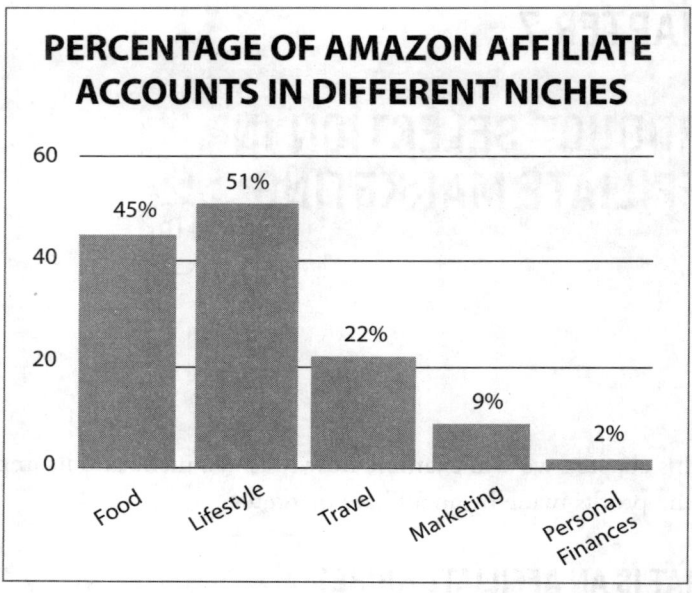

Figure 7.1: Percentage of Amazon Affiliate Accounts in Different Niches

Source: https://brandongaille.com/blog-income-report-st (accessed on 12 July 2019).

you are about it and how much knowledge you have about it. The more interested and skilful you are, the better will be your content. However, there are some other factors also which affect niche selection as given in Figure 7.2. Let us go through each factor in detail.

Problems and Passion

'Inside every problem lies an opportunity.'

Affiliate marketers want to reach a sizeable audience who are ready to spend their hard-earned money on buying their products. And this happens only when there is a dire need for the customer to get rid of a problem they are facing. People are ready to invest in pursuing their passion; it just takes some effort to ignite the fire in them to buy the product which fulfils their passion.

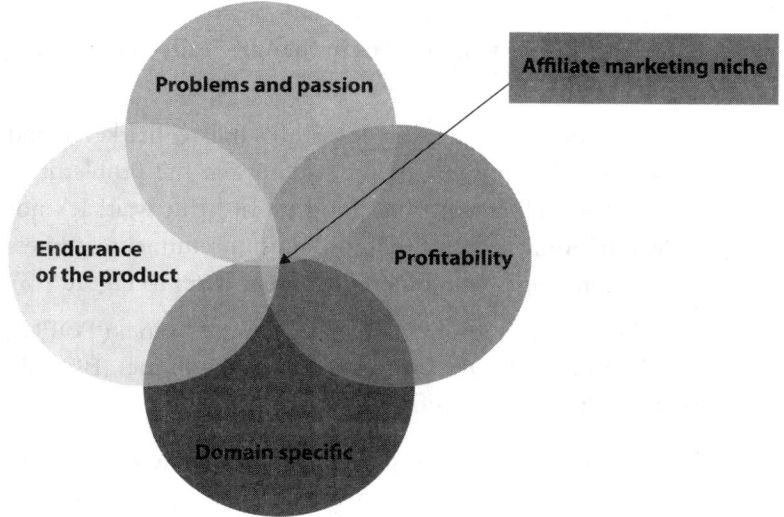

Figure 7.2: Factors Influencing Niche Selection
Source: https://alphainvestors.com/wp-content/uploads/2019/08/affiliate-marekting-niche.jpg (accessed on 12 July 2019).

There are plethora of niches based on problems such as health and wellness, financial management and beauty. People love spending time on pursuing passion and leisure activities. A study shows that people prefer to pursue leisure activities on an average of 7 hours/day (excluding sleeping hours).[1] So choosing a niche based on passion and posting relevant content keeps your audience engaged. A typical example of this niche would be gaming. Many gamers stream their video game online through Twitch; review the latest games in the market and analyse the plethora of equipment and devices which can contribute to a better gaming experience. Gamers around the world record their gameplay and put it up in the Twitch platform for viewers to access. So when enthusiastic visitors click on the affiliate links and purchase, the affiliate gets a commission.

---

[1] https://www.brighthousefinancial.com/education/retirement-planning/passions-planning-and-income-key-insights-for-retirement/ (accessed on 12 July 2019).

Now, let's consider an example of a niche based on problems. As per a report, one in every six persons in the UK is affected by some level of hearing loss.

This is your opportunity to step in as an affiliate marketer and promote hearing aid products, thereby addressing the problems of your customer as well as enjoying good profits. But wait! It's not that simple, is it? Affiliates must follow a customer funnel to address people in different stages with different content (refer to Figure 7.3).

Figure 7.3 shows three regions, namely top of the funnel (TOFU), middle of the funnel (MOFU) and bottom of the funnel (BOFU). Let's briefly analyse their significance.

- **TOFU (cold traffic):** This stage targets people who are aware of their problems but are not aware of the available solutions, including your product. Product reviews and comparison videos belong to this category, as they aid the visitors in revealing the best products available in the market and how far they are suitable to address their problem. For example, a customer has an issue with hearing, and they are oblivious to the products in the market, which could help them solve the problem.

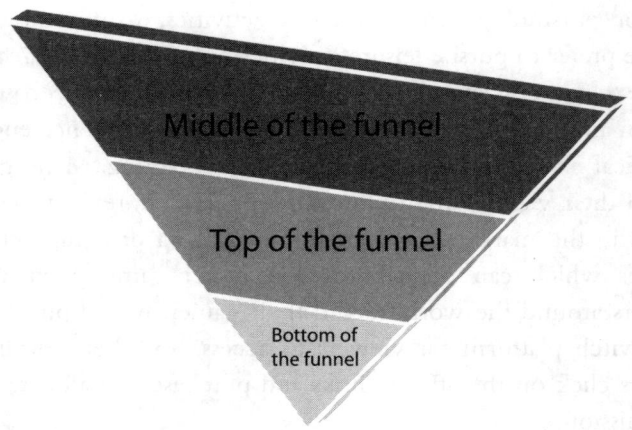

Figure 7.3: Different Stages of the Customer Funnel

Source: https://www.hearinglink.org/your-hearing/about-hearing/facts-about-deafness-hearing-loss/ (accessed on 12 July 2019).

- **MOFU (warm traffic):** This stage targets people who have problems and are aware of the solutions. As an affiliate marketer, your role is to furnish content which tells on what factors they should base their purchase decision so that it solves their problem. For example, the customer knows that they need to buy a hearing aid. Still, an affiliate can inform about the criteria for decision-making such as styles, noise reduction and chargeable batteries.

- **BOFU (hot traffic):** In this stage, people know about the solutions as well as your product. Your content catering to this audience should essentially explain why the product you promote is the best solution in the market. This stage will consist of affiliate links which will drive the visitors to the merchant site. As an affiliate for a hearing aid, you must highlight the unique selling proposition and what differentiates your brand from others.

As an affiliate marketer, it is recommended to cater to all the three stages of the funnel. While the TOFU will give you volume, BOFU will provide you with conversions. Most of the smartphone influencers use these techniques. They keep updating their audience about the newly launched products in the market and their reviews (cold traffic), along with videos showing what people should look (factors) for in a smartphone (warm traffic). These influencers also put out videos about which smartphone is the best in its segment and why (hot traffic).

Profitability

To ensure you receive a fair commission, you must consider the profitability associated with the chosen product. By profitability, we mean the magnitude of money you can make by promoting the product.

While the number of search volume in the niche indicates the demand and pull for the category, the CPC indicates how much marketers are willing to spend on a visit to the landing page. Figure 7.4 shows the search engine results of 'best travel products'.

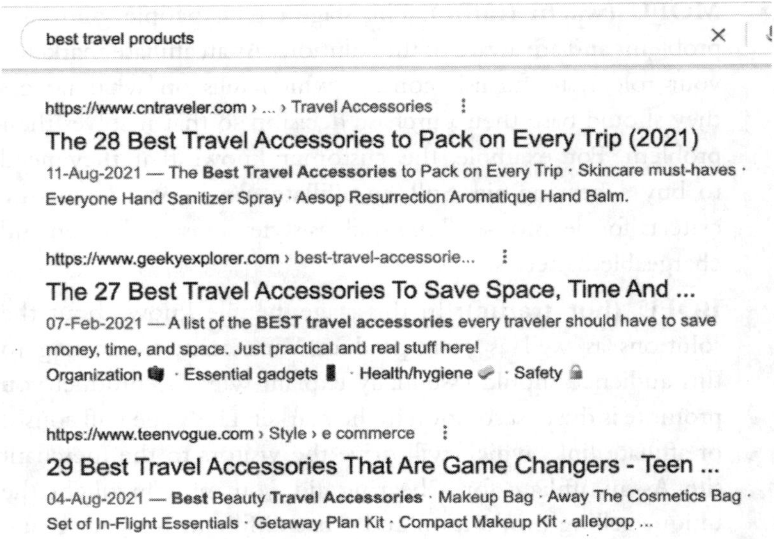

> **best travel products**
>
> https://www.cntraveler.com › ... › Travel Accessories
> ### The 28 Best Travel Accessories to Pack on Every Trip (2021)
> 11-Aug-2021 — The **Best Travel Accessories** to Pack on Every Trip · Skincare must-haves · Everyone Hand Sanitizer Spray · Aesop Resurrection Aromatique Hand Balm.
>
> https://www.geekyexplorer.com › best-travel-accessorie...
> ### The 27 Best Travel Accessories To Save Space, Time And ...
> 07-Feb-2021 — A list of the **BEST travel accessories** every traveler should have to save money, time, and space. Just practical and real stuff here!
> Organization · Essential gadgets · Health/hygiene · Safety
>
> https://www.teenvogue.com › Style › e commerce
> ### 29 Best Travel Accessories That Are Game Changers - Teen ...
> 04-Aug-2021 — **Best** Beauty **Travel Accessories** · Makeup Bag · Away The Cosmetics Bag · Set of In-Flight Essentials · Getaway Plan Kit · Compact Makeup Kit · alleyoop ...

Figure 7.4: Screen Grab of Search Engine Results of 'Best Travel Products'

Source: Google.com

You must then scroll down to the end of the search results page and take a close look at the 'Related Searches' section, as shown in Figure 7.5. These results are the potential topics for your niche from which you can choose the products you wish to promote.

After taking a glance at the 'Related Searches', Affiliates copy all the keywords and move to a keyword tool such as 'Google Keyword Planner' to check if this niche is worth marketing. They analyse the search volume (number of monthly searches in Google) and check one of the columns named 'CPC' or cost per click. It is nothing but the money which advertisers have to pay for a click on the Google Ads for the keyword. Well, CPC doesn't have much to do with affiliate marketing, but the purpose of the above discussion is to understand how CPC gives you an idea about the niche's profitability. Higher CPC means that advertisers are making quite a lot of money by promoting the product.

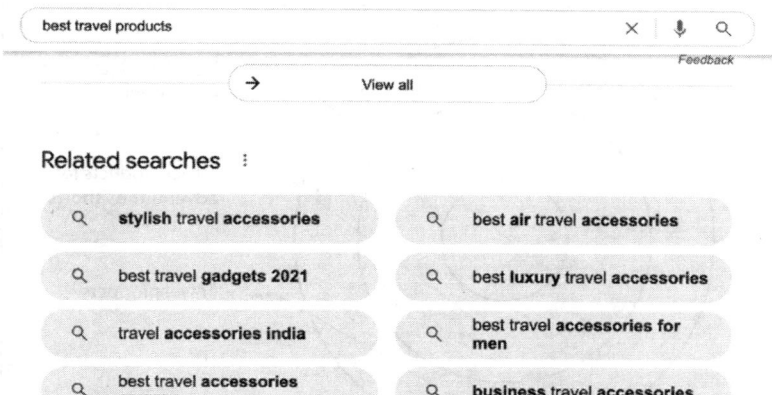

Figure 7.5: Screen Grab of Related Searches' Section

Source: Google.com

A lot of affiliate marketers cross-check on popular affiliate networks (marketplace) such as ClickBank to further ensure that their choice of niche is profitable.

Being Domain-specific

'Travel products' cannot be a niche, as it is too broad and has a lot of subdomains in it which cater to specific sets of audience. Maybe 'travel products for trekking' could be a niche, as it targets a particular group of people. Remember that your niche shouldn't be too narrow that you are left with very few people to target.

Your objective should be to excel in the niche and then explore growth opportunities. You can follow a two-step approach to expansion. The first step is by growing in adjacent niches.

In simple words, if you're initially promoting 'travel products for trekking', then you can very well expand your prowess in promoting 'travel products for skydiving'. The main advantage of this technique is that you have established your credibility as an affiliate marketer in one niche. Then you diversify to another niche, which entices a fair amount of new visitors to your site.

The second step is to promote niches which are supersets, so you move from subset niches to superset niches.

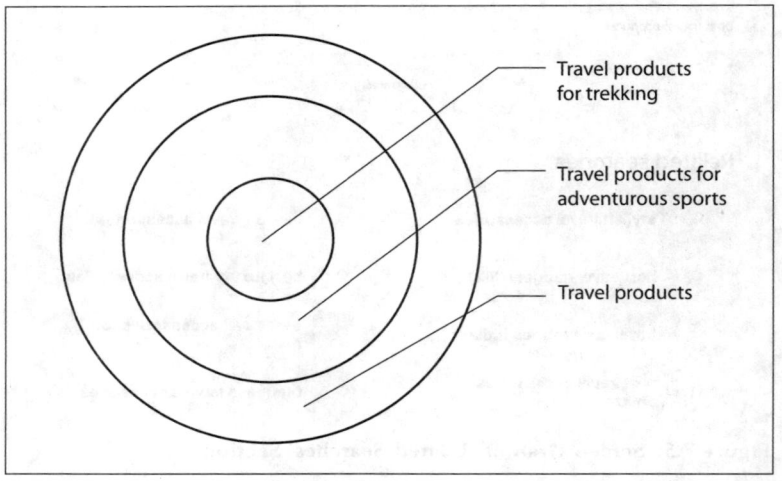

Figure 7.6: Superset and Subset

Figure 7.6 pictorially depicts travel products. It is a superset of travel products for adventure sports which in turn is a superset of travel sports for trekking.

Hence, to scale your business, over a period of time, you can move from travel products for trekking to travel products for adventurous sports. Once you have gained success in it, you can move to travel products, as the business volume will be higher in the broader niche.[2]

Once already established in adjacent niches of say trekking, skydiving and paragliding, you have earned the trust of the reader, thereby making your expansion into the superset of adventure sports a facile task (Figure 7.7).

So why do we promote closely related niches in the first place? Well, the idea is to drive traffic to your site so that you have an excellent array of opportunities lined up to be monetized. And this only happens when you promote niches which are adjacent or supersets.

---

[2] https://twomonkeystravelgroup.com/travel-bloggers-earning-5000-usd-month-monetize-blogs-2/ (accessed on 7 December 2021).

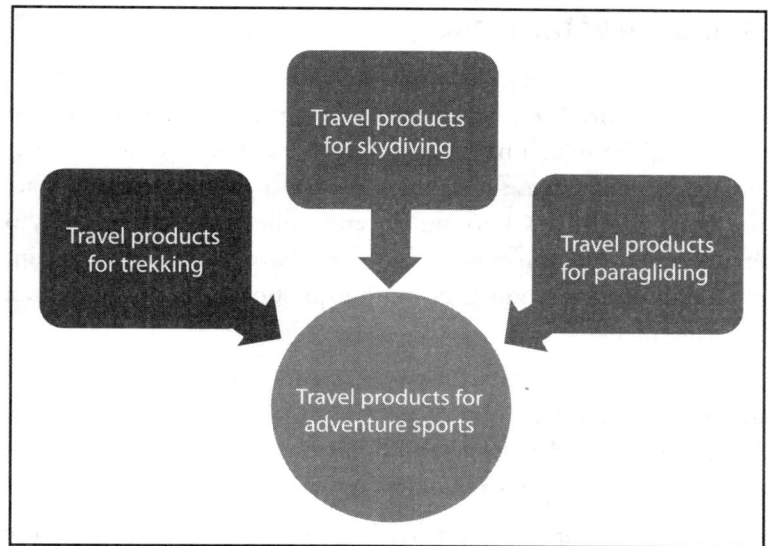

Figure 7.7: Adjacent Niches and Superset Niches

Many affiliate marketers have efficiently monetized through this technique and became stalwarts in their niche. A popular name in travel blogs is Matthew Kepnes, alias Nomadic Matt. On average, Matthew makes about $50,000 per month from his travel blogs, to which affiliate marketing is one of the vital contributors.[3]

The homepage of a popular travel blog nomadicmatt.com show categories in the menu, such as 'Resources' and 'Shop' under which affiliate marketing is done.

A similar example in the Indian context would be Anuradha Goyal. She runs a travel blog by the name Indiatales. After starting as a travel blogger, she has been promoting products through her blogs. She reviews hotels, restaurants and products as an affiliate marketer. Once again, it takes perseverance to establish a blog with interrelated niche, and that's the most challenging part as an affiliate marketer.

---

[3] https://www.nomadicmatt.com/ (accessed on 12 July 2019).

Endurance of the Niche

No one wants to invest their time and resources in a niche which is a fad or short-lived. If you are a beginner, you are advised to choose a niche which has been around for a while, so that you get adequate customer base and time to establish yourself in the affiliate marketing industry. Choosing an enduring niche allows you to set up a stable business as you do not have the time constraint in promoting the product. Now, the question is: How to find an enduring niche?

We can take the help of Google Trends to answer the above question. Google Trends analyses the popularity of search queries about the keyword that we enter. We can view the search trends over time across various regions as well.

As an affiliate marketer, you need to take into consideration the popularity over a period of time or, in simple words, the endurance of your niche before choosing it.

In this chapter, we have discussed the factors you should consider for choosing a niche. In the next chapter, we will be exploring some ubiquitous affiliate networks.

CHAPTER 8

LEVERAGING AFFILIATE NETWORKS

This chapter will throw light on the affiliate network and its importance and how to choose a network. It will provide an overview of some of the major affiliate networks such as ClickBank. The chapter will also discuss some big affiliate programmes—Amazon Associates and Flipkart Affiliate—so that you can kick-start your affiliate journey.

WHAT IS AN AFFILIATE NETWORK?

We can see from Figure 8.1 that Amazon Associates holds 39.3 per cent of the market share in the affiliate network. This immense market share is attributed to the enormous consumer base of Amazon and its huge variety of products, thus providing wide opportunities to affiliates.

WHY AFFILIATE NETWORK?

Let us discuss the importance of affiliate networks for merchants as well as publishers.

Merchant's Perspective

- The top priority for any merchant is sales or leads. Affiliate networks help merchants increase their sales, as they have a large number of affiliates in these networks.

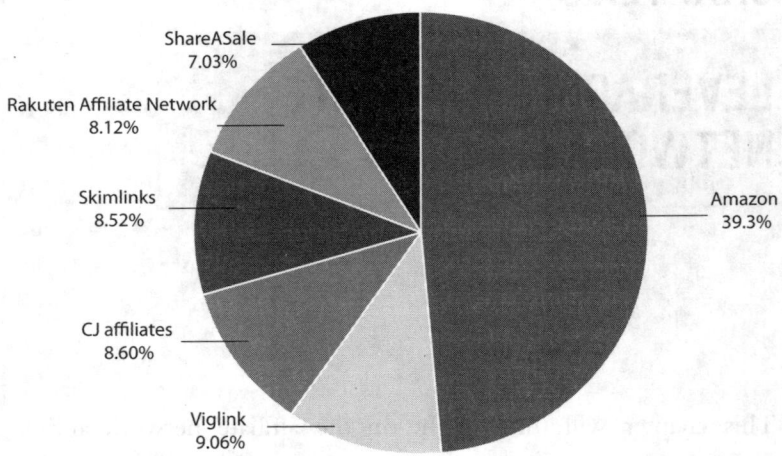

Figure 8.1: Market Share of Popular Affiliate Networks in 2019
Source: https://www.datanyze.com/market-share/affiliate-networks (accessed on 10 December 2019).

- These networks ease the burden of creating content, generating leads and acquiring customers so that merchants can invest time and resources in enhancing their brand image and product quality.

Publisher's Perspective

- As a beginner in the field of affiliate marketing, these networks would provide you with exposure to different affiliate products in the market, thereby giving you a kick-start in the field of affiliate marketing.
- Since affiliate networks have an enormous array of products, the affiliate has a plethora of products to make money from.

POPULAR AFFILIATE NETWORKS

Let us discuss some of the popular affiliate networks which have a good reputation in the market.

ClickBank

ClickBank is a popular name in affiliate networks. Although it doesn't have a significant market share, the reputation it has built over the years attracts a lot of customers. With sales worth $3 billion, ClickBank has grown to be one of the leading retailers to serve over 200 million people and 6 million entrepreneurs across 190 nations.[1]

ClickBank is so popular and preferred by budding affiliates because of the high commission that it pays (up to 75%). Figure 8.2 provides us with an insight into the industries where ClickBank holds a prowess.

As we can see from Figure 8.2, health is the biggest industry with 5 per cent popularity on ClickBank. But the exciting part is that 86.8 per cent of the industries belong to the miscellaneous category, which shows the outreach of ClickBank across sectors.

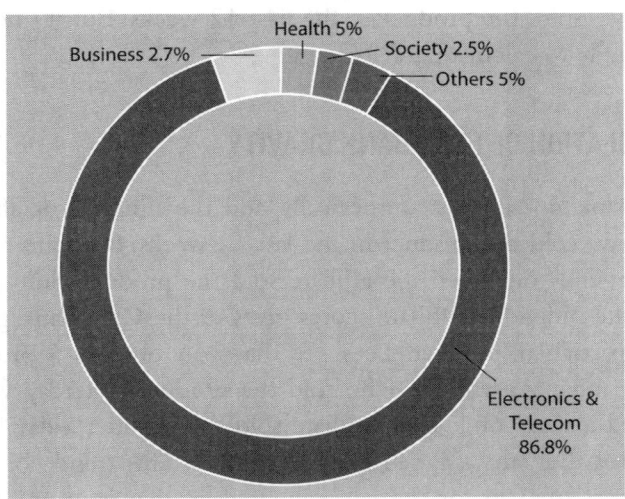

Figure 8.2: ClickBank's Share of Industries

Source: https://www.Clickbank.com/affiliate-network/ (accessed on 10 December 2019).

---

[1] https://www.Clickbank.com/corp/our-story/ (accessed on 10 December 2019).

In ClickBank, there are three main metrics you should consider as an affiliate before promoting any product.

1. **Initial $/sale:** This is the primary metric an affiliate considers, as it gives the average amount of money an affiliate makes per sale. For example, $50 as 'initial $/sale' means that on average, affiliates make around $50 as commission for each sale of that product.

2. **Average percentage sale:** This metric gives us the average percentage of the selling price which the affiliate receives as commission. So let's say that the 'average percentage sale' for the product in the previous example is 70 per cent. This means that a $50 commission earned by the affiliate is 70 per cent of the selling price. This gives an idea about the selling price, which is $71.42, and also the magnitude of commission one can expect by promoting the product.

3. **Gravity:** This is the total number of distinct affiliates who have sold the product in the past 12 weeks. But it's not that simple to calculate gravity.[2]

CALCULATION OF CLICKBANK GRAVITY

ClickBank doesn't just numerically add the number of affiliates who have sold the product in the last 12 weeks. It assigns a score that depends on when the affiliate sold the product. Summation of all the individual affiliate scores gives us the ClickBank gravity for a particular product. Let's say that you observe a product's gravity today. An affiliate who sold the product yesterday will be assigned a score of 1. If an affiliate sold the product a day before yesterday, they are assigned a score of 0.96. This trend continues in powers of 0.96 for the subsequent days; that is, if an affiliate sold the product (number of products sold doesn't matter) 'x' days back, then the affiliate score assigned to them is $0.96^{(x-1)}$. Once

---

[2] https://www.similartech.com/technologies/Clickbank-affiliate./ (accessed on 10 December 2019).

again, remember that the 'days' here refers to the day you check the ClickBank gravity. So don't be shocked to see a different gravity tomorrow! Affiliates, in general, prefer to promote a product if the gravity is above 20.

vCommission

vCommission established in 2008 is a well-known name in the Indian affiliate market. It is India's leading affiliate network, delivering performance to top Indian brands through a growing network of 17,500 affiliates.

vCommission has a proper process of selecting competent affiliates for its network. You need to provide your bank account number and PAN number, along with necessary information such as name, email and phone number.

Moreover, you must have a website with a certain number of visitors to get approved. After submitting your details for verification, it takes at least three–seven days to get approval.

Most of the affiliate networks pay commission on the same models with minor changes.

- CPA: Cost per action (the affiliate network will mention action)
- CPS: Cost per sale
- EPM: Earning per 1,000 impressions
- EPC: Earning per click
- CTR: Click-through rate (number of clicks for every 100 impressions)
- OSC: On-site conversions (number of sales for every 100 impressions or actions)

You need to look for CPA offers before starting the promotions. These offers can vary from ₹10 to ₹200. Also, you need to check the offer's expiry date. CPA can be for subscription, click, install, sale, etc. You need approval for the kind of promotion that you are going to use. They thoroughly check your request before allowing you to promote, as they don't want any wrong kind of promotion.

vCommission also provides you with performance reports. The platform allows you to filter the information on any criterion and get the report the way you want it. It also allows you to track commission earned through conversions and referrals.

You can choose to receive your commission either through direct bank transfer or through PayPal. The threshold income that vCommission pays you is $100 (currently around ₹7,500). So you need to earn at least $100 for vCommission to hand you your earnings. They pay you once on a 30-day cycle. Also, vCommission takes some part of your earnings as their commission.

vCommission is a serious affiliate network which believes in providing quality service to both the parties involved. So you can't afford to take their rules casually, as they immediately ban people if something is wrong. Also, as the platform contains many experienced affiliates, it can get stressful at times, especially for beginners.

Some of the popular merchants that vCommission has are Amazon, Expedia, Travel Guru, Naaptol, Paytm, OLX, Axis Bank Home Loan, Kotak Mahindra Bank, Domino's, Zivame and MobiKwik.

Cuelinks

Cuelinks is a content monetization tool for bloggers, deal site owners, coupon sites, forum owners or any publisher which sends outbound traffic to online shopping, travel, finance or matrimony websites. It allows you to automatically monetize your content by identifying SEO keywords in your content and adding affiliate links within your content.

Important things to know about Cuelinks are as follows:

- Minimum payout is ₹500.

- Revenue-sharing percentage is 75:25 between a publisher (you, in this case) and Cuelinks.

- By default, Cuelinks monetizes all the merchant links they are associated with. In case, you want to work directly with any particular merchant (e.g., Amazon affiliate), you can convey it to the Cuelinks team, and they will remove Amazon from your account.

Cuelinks offers programmes with Airtel, Amazon India, BabyOye, Chumbak, Domino's, eBay India, FabIndia, Flipkart, Freecharge, Jabong, ShopClues, Snapdeal and over other 600+ merchants.

Cuelinks is excellent for any Indian blog whose target audience is Indian or getting traffic from India. It saves your time for signing up separately for an individual affiliate programme. You need to search for any affiliate programme in the merchant lookup menu in the Cuelinks dashboard and provide the link of the product from that affiliate site.

CUELINKS WIDGETS

You can add widgets with coupons for the big stores to your blog sidebar. To create this widget, click on Resource Center → Widgets and generate the widget according to your blog.

CUEWORDS

This tool helps you by converting text to links. It gives you the option to control how many words on a page it should transform into affiliate links. It recommends that you keep the limit below five, as anything more than that can compromise viewers' experience.

CJ Affiliate

If you have an established audience and you want a feature-rich affiliate network then you should go with CJ Affiliate. However, it may not be a good choice for beginners. Because accounts are deactivated if you go six months without earning a commission, and because their merchants have a reputation for being picky on who they accept as publishers, CJ Affiliate is best for those who get steady traffic to their websites.

Rakuten

If you want an affiliate network with an intuitive user interface, a great reporting system, then you can try Rakuten. Rakuten Marketing (formerly LinkShare) has been hooking up merchants and publishers for over two decades and hence is a very trustworthy network.

ShareASale

Anyone who's looking for a reliable affiliate network which offers a wide variety of affiliate marketing options should give ShareASale a try. ShareASale will eliminate the need to join multiple networks. Currently, I am using ShareASale, as it covers most of my preferences.

So now I will tell you everything you need to know to start earing money from scratch. How to create an account? Since we are the affiliates, we need to sign up to create an affiliate account. An important point here to know is that you need to have a website to sign up on ShareASale.

CREATING AN ACCOUNT IN AFFILIATE NETWORKS

You can go ahead and create an account on ShareASale. So the next step is to look for the merchants and the products that we want to promote.

For that, on the home page, we will go to Merchants → Search for merchants.

The most intuitive thing to do now is to browse the product categories given in the left. Ranging from online services such as web hosting and email marketing to physical goods such as clothes and books, ShareASale has got it all covered.

The number written alongside the product category displays the number of products available in this category.

Let's take an example of general web services for now. There are 68 products under this category. You might be thinking that it will be a cumbersome task to look for the best products among these. Right! But we are lucky to have a product sorting algorithm. We can sort product on the basis of the following categories. I will explain all these one by one.

1. **Power rank:** Knowing which merchants are having the most success on the platform can help you uncover profitable niches. Fortunately, ShareASale tells us which of its merchants are performing well through its power rank.

2. **EPC:** Seven-day EPC is a calculation made by taking data from yesterday, counting back seven days. We take the sum of all commissions for the 7 days and divide it by the sum of all clicks for the same 7 days, then multiplying this by 100.

3. For instance, let's say a seller sets the cookie duration to 30 days. This means that affiliates have exactly 30 days to seal the deal, once a link has been clicked. Once this time is up, that's it—no profit for you. However, if a purchase is made within this period, it qualifies for a commission.

4. Moreover, if you want to play it safe, you can sort the result on the basis of the joining date. The older the product, the more trust it gains.

Then we also have other parameters such as alphabetical order, sale commission and lead commission.

If you are a beginner, then power rank can prove to be one of the easiest methods to pick up the right products to promote.

Before applying to any affiliate programme, one of the most important steps is to check the status history of the product. It gives you a breakdown about the number of days in which the merchant was online. If the number of days when the merchant is offline and has low funds is high, then you should avoid applying to such programmes.

Once you are confident about the product, you can apply for it by clicking on the join programme CTA.

While some programmes have an instant approval, there are products which might take up to 10–15 days to get the approval.

HOW TO FETCH LINKS FROM AFFILIATE NETWORKS

Once you have got approval from your favourite product, the next step is to promote it on your website. To promote the approved products, we need to go to Links → Get links/banners.

Now, the most crucial step is to fetch the affiliate links. If you are writing a review or a comparison article, then you can add these affiliate links in between the article. Just click on the text links and then you will see a table. This table comprises of a unique link id, a brief description and the category of the link.

We cannot directly copy the affiliate link in between our articles, as it will look odd. So we usually hyperlink the anchor text, and here is an example.

In my SEMrush article, I have used the anchor text 'Curious Where You Rank in Google'. So whenever someone will click this text, they will be taken directly to the SEMrush website.

Now, let's fetch the link; for that, click on 'get HTML code'.

Now you have two options: One is to copy the HTML code and the other is to copy the URL only; you can choose this according to your convenience.

You might be wondering that how will the merchant know that which customers are sent by me? Let's have a look at the URL. Here in the URL, this is the link ID, merchant ID and the unique user ID: u= 2637300. Through this unique ID, the merchant will know which customers are sent by us. And finally, we will get the commission accordingly.

Another way to promote the products is by using an attractive banner ad. You can read my article on banner ads on my website to know more about these banner ads. There are different types and sizes offered by various merchants.

Here, I have used a banner ad of 300 × 250 on my SEMrush review article. Another point to know is that these banner ads also contain our affiliate link, so if someone will click on this banner, then also we will get commissions.

We also create custom links in case we want to take the user to a specific page on the product website.

Similarly, we can fetch videos; although only a few merchants offer videos, videos are capable of generating instant conversions, as the visitors can get an idea about the product in a couple of seconds. You can fetch the video width according to your own preferences as well.

HOW TO ANALYSE YOUR PERFORMANCE

Our primal goal for joining an affiliate programme is to earn money through our insightful content. But how will you know whether you were able to influence your readers or not? The good part is that ShareASale provides in-depth reports about your various affiliate products. Let's dig a little deeper.

First, click on reports, so that we can generate a merchant summary; daily, weekly and monthly reports; traffic reports, etc. Let's discuss the significance of these reports and how these reports play a critical role in determining your future decisions.

Say I had written a review article on SEMrush, so let's see its traffic report. Now I will select my merchant—SEMrush—sort the results by unique hits, as I am interested in that. Whenever a user clicks on my affiliate link, it will count as one unique hit. Suppose I get 10 unique hits, then it means that 10 different users have clicked my affiliate link. We can also select a specific date range as well. Now let's click on filter results.

In the traffic report, we can see the number of hits on different banners. We can find the banners with maximum number of clicks. We can also know the anchor text we have used here. It is 'Curious Where You Rank in Google? Find Out Here!' So we can infer that most users are interested in this feature of SEMrush. Now, the benefit of knowing this is that in future if we want to promote SEMrush through email marketing or LinkedIn posts, we will give emphasis to the website ranking feature of SEMrush.

Now suppose that in accordance with our niche, we can promote email marketing products, web hosting products and other online web services. After getting a wider view of the reports we can know which category of products is giving us better results so that we can choose our new merchants more wisely.

AMAZON ASSOCIATES

With 39 per cent of the market share in affiliate networks, Amazon Associates is one of the most preferred affiliate programmes.[3]

Creating an Amazon Affiliate Account

It is free to sign up for Amazon Associates, but you need an active website or a blog or be active enough on any social media platform. The following is the step-by-step process to create an Amazon affiliate account.

Firstly, you have to visit the Amazon Associate homepage and click on 'Join Now', which will redirect you to the Amazon login page. After logging in, enter your details.

Now, you have to enter the address of your website/blog/YouTube channel. Remember that having an engaging website is beneficial. You have to now choose a preferred user ID or 'store ID'. After that, explain what your website is all about and select the product domains which you wish to sell through your website.

Now, you will have to mention how you would drive traffic through your website. The portal asks you to tick options you deem fit. Your website won't get approved if it doesn't attract a decent amount of traffic. So self-evaluate your website before applying for it.

Then there would be a verification step, wherein the portal asks you to enter your phone number, and as you press the 'call me now' tab, you will get a call from Amazon instructing to enter a four-digit pin.

[3] https://blog.hubspot.com/sales/amazon-affiliate (accessed on 10 December 2019).

Lastly, you have to choose a suitable payment method. That's it! You are ready to go as an Amazon affiliate. But wait, not so early. Next comes the affiliate link generation part.

Generating the Affiliate Link

An affiliate link is a link through which the customer has to reach the merchant site and purchase the product. You must understand how the affiliate link functions, how to make affiliate links readable and how the merchant site identifies unique affiliate links. The following flow chart shows how an affiliate link works and its role in affiliate marketing (Figure 8.3).

For getting the tailored link for an Amazon product, you need to access https://affiliate- program.amazon.com/home and search for

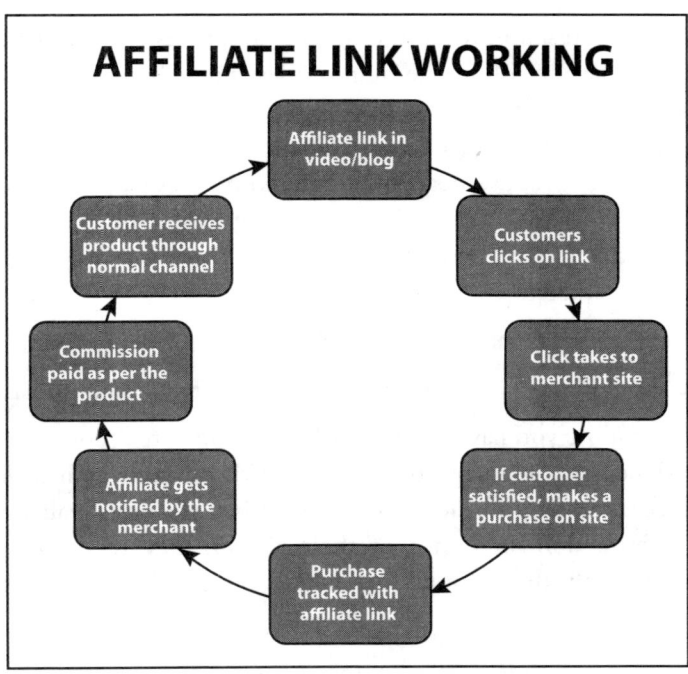

Figure 8.3: Flow Chart of How Amazon Affiliate Link Works

any product which you wish to market. After receiving relevant search results, you are supposed to click on 'Get Link'.

A window will flash on the screen with your affiliate link tailored for the specific product you clicked on. You can copy and paste the link on your website. You can also shorten your links.[4]

Customizing Links

On clicking 'Get Link', you will get some choices related to the visual appeal of the link. You can choose a text link, an image link or a combination of both text and image.

Some customization can also be done by changing the colour of the background, title and price.

These customized links are tailored for your affiliate ID and the product you wish to promote. So the merchant knows exactly which affiliate is driving sales of which product.

We have discussed in detail the signing-up process. So, what next? Well, you have to follow the thumb rules and techniques discussed in the previous chapters to be successful as an Amazon affiliate. The factors we have discussed are universal and apply to all affiliate networks. As a consumer, you might know about the lucrative discounts Amazon offers during the festive season, be it Diwali or Black Friday. So you must take advantage of these to make the most of it as a marketer.

As an Amazon affiliate, you must consider using a genius link.

Why should I use Geniuslink? Why not the affiliate link directly?

Let us suppose you have created an Amazon affiliate account in the India-based site. If international users click on your affiliate link, the link takes them to the Amazon site. When the users realize that the website domain is not of their region, they tend to open Amazon with their country domain and purchase. You won't

---

[4] https://www.business2community.com/affiliate-marketing/everything-you-need-to-know-about-amazons-affiliate-program-02246561 (accessed on 7 December 2019).

be receiving any commission if this happens. To curb this, you have two options:

1. You create an individual affiliate account in each of the 11 international sites and share all the links in your post. This is a cumbersome process and does not provide a good user experience.

2. That's why we recommend that you use Geniuslink.

Geniuslink identifies the geography of your website visitors, then sends them to the specific Amazon page of that particular country.

Geniuslink makes life easy by detecting the customers' country, language preference and other factors and directs them to the best web page suitable for the particular customer. One more important feature in Geniuslink is that you can add a tracking 'pixel' to each of your affiliate links, so that you can track the customer and build a custom audience for remarketing.[5]

But why do we need to add pixels?

With this data, you can run a remarketing campaign on Facebook or Google, targeting people who had earlier clicked on your link and shown interest in the products you are promoting.[6]

When you showcase your content to an engaged audience as well as those who are having similar interests, you will get better conversions.[7]

Commission Structure for Amazon Associates

Amazon doesn't provide lucrative commissions like ClickBank or any other affiliate network, yet many affiliates choose Amazon Associates, keeping in mind the large trusted customer base of

---

[5] https://www.smartpassiveincome.com/guide/affiliate-marketing-strategies/affiliate-marketing-amazon/ (accessed on 11 December 2019).

[6] https://www.geni.us/ (accessed on 11 December 2019).

[7] https://blog.geni.us/take-your-affiliate-links-to-the-next-level-with-retargeting-pixels/ (accessed on 11 December 2019).

Amazon. The maximum commission you could earn is 10 per cent of the selling price. A vital part of Amazon affiliates is that they can make money even when the user doesn't buy the promoted product through their link. Yeah, you read it right! If the customer clicks on your link and then buys a different product other than the promoted product, you'll still be paid the commission for the product purchased. This scheme is valid for 24 hours after the user clicks on your affiliate link and arrives at the Amazon site. For understanding, let's take an example. Assume that you're promoting a watch as an Amazon associate, and the viewer is impressed by your content and clicks on your affiliate link. For some reason, the user changes their mind and buys another commodity, say a wallet. In this case, you'll receive a commission for the wallet being purchased.

You will receive a commission, even if the user adds some other product in the cart within 24 hours and buys the same before the cart expires (typically 90 days).[8]

Also, there are rules and regulations that you must follow. Amazon doesn't allow you to use the affiliate links in any offline manner, which includes email marketing, e-books, printed material, etc. Also, you need to explicitly mention it to your website visitors that you will earn a commission when they make a purchase using your link. The Amazon Associates Program offers detailed reports of clicks on your affiliate links, earnings, conversion rate and details of orders placed using your links such as shipping and delivery status. If any of the orders placed using your link is returned, then the earnings will be deducted from your account.

Amazon pays you every month. Also, the payment for each month is made 60 days after the end of the month. You can receive your compensation via a cheque or into your account through NEFT (National Electronic Funds Transfer).

---

[8] https://affiliate-program.amazon.in/help/operating/schedule (accessed on 14 December 2019).

Amazon mandates minimum earnings of ₹2,500 to issue a cheque and a minimum of ₹1,000 to deposit the money in your account via NEFT. Do note that the Amazon affiliate programme regularly works on filtering the underperforming associates. Every associate is required to refer at least three sales within 180 days of getting an affiliate account. Failing to do so will lead to the elimination of your account.

We advise you to not rely solely on Amazon associates for your affiliate income. You must diversify and keep a bag of options to have a steady flow of income. You must sign up for other affiliate networks (such as vCommission and ShareASale) or programmes (such as eBay Network, Flipkart Network and Apple Network). We also know that Amazon doesn't provide the most lucrative commission like other networks; so experienced affiliates always aim to diversify in the field by signing up for multiple networks which will supplement their income.

Pros and Cons of Being an Amazon Affiliate

We have seen that Amazon associates have a lot of advantages. Let us summarize the key pros of being an Amazon affiliate.

PROS

- It is easy breezy to get started as an Amazon affiliate.
- Due to its massive brand reputation and reliability, the affiliates need not break a sweat in alluring customers to purchase from Amazon.
- It offers an enormous number of affiliate products to choose (close to 3 billion) within any niche.
- The 24-hour window for buying any product after clicking on the link and adding items to the cart and buying before it expires can augment your earnings significantly.

Let us take an overview of the cons of being an Amazon affiliate.

CONS

- Amazon's commissions can be very disappointing at times. For example, you won't be paid any cut if a consumer buys gift cards, video gaming consoles and Prime membership.
- Often, budding affiliates find it difficult to apprehend the Amazon Associates programme operating agreement. Due to frequent updates in the policies, beginners have to be more careful.
- Not running a website beforehand can be a disadvantage in getting your account approved.

FLIPKART AFFILIATE PROGRAM

Well, the process of becoming a member of the Flipkart Affiliate Program isn't very different from the process of being an Amazon associate, apart from the commission and the way Flipkart pays the commission to the affiliates.

Flipkart offers you two ways to receive payments from your affiliate programme.

Electronic Fund Transfer

In this method, the money will be transferred into your account once it reaches a threshold limit. If you opt for electronic funds transfer (EFT), then you need to provide your account details along with a picture of a cancelled cheque.

If you don't have an account, you can use someone else's account details. The minimum threshold limit for EFT is ₹5,000.

Electronic Gift Voucher

You can also use your earnings in the form of gift vouchers while buying products from Flipkart. The minimum amount of earnings to get gift vouchers is ₹2,500. All you need to do is to give your address proof. This method can be used by those who don't have a bank account.

What's exciting about the Flipkart's programme is the tools it offers.

API

It is one of the most beneficial tools of the Flipkart Affiliate Program. It can be used in price comparison articles, coupon sites, etc. It helps you to write an article which will automatically update the prices when it changes on Flipkart.

If you have displayed prices without Flipkart API, then you will have to update every time the price changes, which can be challenging.

PRODUCT LINK AND BANNERS

Flipkart lets you customize the links and banners the way you want so that it looks similar to the layout and colour scheme of your site.

1. Text colour
2. Link colour
3. Background colour
4. Price info (on/off)
5. Content border (on/off)

PROMOTIONAL BANNER AND WIDGETS

These tools provide updated information on your website. They can also be customized and made interactive.

After choosing one of the options, all you need to do is select the option of 'Generate the code' and add that code to your website.

SEARCH TOOLS

This allows your website visitors to search through Flipkart directly. This eliminates a situation where the visitor leaves your website, thus increasing your chances of conversion.

For example, you wrote an article about how amazing the new Galaxy Z is, but your users find the product quite expensive. Then, the tool allows them to search for alternatives directly from your site.

By doing this, you are providing an extensive range of products to your users, and since they will click on all these products through your link, your chances of earning a commission increase.

While Flipkart offers an ample number of creative tools, it is stricter than Amazon. As per the rules of the Flipkart Affiliate Program, you will earn a commission only when the visitor buys a product within the session time or adds it to their cart, which is just 30 minutes. A session starts when a visitor clicks on the link of your website and ends when either they add the product into the cart or the session of 30 minutes expires.

If the product added into your cart is removed, your commission gets cancelled. Also, Flipkart has a 30-day refund policy, so it takes typically 30–45 days to receive your commission.

Unlike the Amazon affiliate programme, Flipkart doesn't have any verification process for its affiliates. This makes it an excellent platform for beginners. While Amazon updates the status on your commission daily, Flipkart updates on weekly, monthly or quarterly basis. We have examined a few networks and programmes in detail; let us review some more affiliate programmes.

POPULAR E-COMMERCE AFFILIATE PROGRAMMES

As the volume of online shopping is increasing, e-commerce is emerging as one of the most popular niches. Some of the best affiliate programmes around e-commerce are as follows.

Flipkart Affiliate Program

- Easy to join for beginners
- One of the major e-commerce sites in India
- The commission is decent, especially for gadgets
- Too strict regulations (only 30-minute session)

Amazon Affiliate Programme

- World leader in e-commerce
- Updates your affiliate account daily (unlike Flipkart)
- Commission offered is average
- Most favourable rules among all (can buy any product within 24 hours of clicking on the link)

eBay Affiliate Programme

- The session lasts for 24 hours (better than Flipkart) Famous outside India (USA)
- Offers lower commission rates (2%–6%)

Let us review some travel affiliate programmes.

OYO Affiliate Programme (OYO Circle)

- Free to join (need to request)
- Payout is rolled out every month
- The commission depends on various factors such as the average booking value and number of bookings. Higher the amount of revenue you generate, higher will be your commission.
- A booking is considered complete after the checkout.

TripAdvisor Affiliate Program

- Minimum of 50 per cent commission
- The commission is earned when the visitor clicks on the link to the hotel booking partner's website (no booking is required)
- It allows a 14-day window, in which, if the visitor returns to the hotel website, even from a different device or channel, the affiliate earns the commission.

MakeMyTrip Affiliate Programme

- India's pioneering online travel portal
- On every domestic flight ticket booked via your link, you can earn around ₹105–₹126. Social media or Facebook ads are not allowed for promotion.

Let us review some fashion affiliate programmes.

Myntra Affiliate Programme

Myntra is one of the leading e-commerce fashion companies. Here are two network aggregators which offer Myntra affiliate programmes:

- **AffZip:** Once you sign up with them, you have to post links in your blogs, websites, etc. If any of your content viewers do any shopping after reaching Myntra through your site, within that cookie duration, you will be paid. For AffZip, cookie duration is 30 days. Creative tools you can use here are banners, coupon codes, deep linking and email newsletters.
- **Cuelinks:** It is the same as AffZip. The only difference is that it has a cookie period of seven days. Here, you can earn a payout of about 3.9–4.68 per cent on every sale.

Fbb Affiliate Programme

- Fbb is India's fashion hub, satisfying fashion enthusiasts across India by providing modern and trendy apparel at pocket-friendly prices. There are a few networks that offer Fbb affiliate programmes such as INRDeals, Cuelinks, AffZip and VigLink.
- INRDeals provides numerous advantages over other sites. It offers pre-approved Fbb affiliate campaigns with detailed category-wise payout structure based on the CPS model. It also gives Super Affiliates direct access to Fbb API.
- The base payout commission rate for Fbb affiliate programme is 9.6 per cent per sale, and it can go up to 12 per cent.

Tata CLiQ Affiliate Programme

- Tata CLiQ is an Indian e-commerce venture (of Tata Group), whose expertise is in selling international luxury brands.
- Cuelinks provide a timely update of every sale, exclusive deals or discount on the Tata CLU affiliate programme.
- For every sale via your link, there is a payout of 6–7.2 per cent. Bulk orders are not allowed.
- Cuelinks does not share commission for coupon, deal or discount.

Let us review some health/fitness/beauty affiliate programmes.

Body Shop

- Cosmetics, skincare and perfume company
- Eight per cent flat commission
- Thirty-day cookie window
- Thirty-day payment terms

Fitbit

- The industry leader in fitness bands
- Three per cent commission rate
- High conversion rates
- Free membership and top tools provided

Medlife Affiliate Program

- You need to be above the age of 18 years
- There is a proper approval process; once signed up, your website will be reviewed for a few days, and then accordingly, approval will be given

- Up to 20 per cent commission on delivery orders
- No subscription fee to join.

Let us review some insurance affiliate programmes

Policybazaar Affiliate Programme

- Policybazaar provides a digital platform to compare the financial services from major insurance companies in India
- You can join this affiliate programme by signing up at INRDeals
- It allows the generation of affiliate links to track transactions online in real-time
- The base affiliate commission payout is ₹112 for every lead; it can be further increased based on volume and can go up to a maximum of ₹140 per lead

Easy Insurance India Affiliate Programme

- Easy Insurance India empowers you to compare the products offered by various insurance companies in one shot
- You will earn money for every visitor from your site who clicks on the link and visits www.easyinsuranceindia.com and registers there

CHAPTER 9

LEARN TO PLAY BY SEO RULES

SEO is one of the foremost techniques through which affiliates earn more profits. In this chapter, you will learn about the algorithm for ranking your pages in search engine results to drive more traffic to your website and increase sales.

WHAT IS SEO?

SEO is the process of increasing the quality and quantity of website traffic by increasing the visibility of a website to users of a web search engine. It is used to leverage organic search results (you need not pay for making your website appear at the top of the search engine results). SEO targets a variety of searches which include image search, video search and vertical domain-specific search.

HOW DOES SEO WORK?

Any search engine (Google, Yahoo or Bing) has a crawler (or search engine bots) which goes out and collects data about every content it finds on the Internet. This process happens in an automated and methodical manner. Crawlers initially discover websites, and using the links on those sites, they discover other web pages as well. Crawlers create a copy of all pages so that they bring back binary data (1s and 0s) to the search engine to build an index, which is nothing but a huge database from which these web pages can be retrieved. In layman's terms, if a web page is not available in the index, then the user cannot find the same in the search results. The search index keeps track of all the signals of websites—from keywords to backlinks. This index is then fed through a complex algorithm which tries to match the data with the query you searched for in the search engine and ranks the pages based on relevance score. And all this happens in a fraction of a second.

The organic search results do not come with any 'ad' tag. Google's search algorithm uses more than 200 factors to rank these websites, in which high-quality content, meta tags and backlinks (we will discuss them in a while) are vital factors for ranking. Google accounts for 75 per cent of the global desktop traffic, outperforming its competitors.[1]

WHY SEO FOR AFFILIATE MARKETING?

Now that you know what SEO is, let's examine why SEO is essential for an affiliate marketer.

- If your website does not appear in the search results, then how would you get the users to your website? A report by Zero Limit Web shows that 67.60 per cent of clicks happen on the first five organic search results only. According to a study, as large as 75 per cent never go to the second page of Google search results, which indicates how vital it is for a website to rank on the first page.[2]

- Around 61 per cent of marketers feel that improving SEO is one of the top marketing strategies. Once your site becomes visible to the audience, then you are left with the job of delivering engaging content catering to your target audience, as discussed in previous chapters. Once users visit the site, the top factors considered by Google to know if the content was relevant are website visits, time spent on the site and bounce

---

[1] https://netmarketshare.com/ (accessed on 12 December 2019).

[2] https://www.zerolimitweb.com/organic-vs-ppc-2019-ctr-results-best-practices/ (accessed on 12 December 2019).

rate (which is the percentage of visitors who enter the site and leave without viewing any other pages within the website).[3]

HOW TO FLOURISH AS AN AFFILIATE MARKETER USING SEO?

SEO is free of cost. Of course, there is the cost of creating content, but you don't have to run paid ads to be visible in the search results. You just need to adopt some techniques to abide by the search engine's algorithm. Let's explore them one by one.

Augment Your Website with the Right Keywords

Often the top search results are very specific to the search query, meaning that as a beginner, you will not stand a chance if you just fill in your website with keywords of high search volume. Instead, what expert affiliate marketers suggest is that you need to choose keywords which are longer and less competitive. For example, it will be challenging for a new website to rank on the first page for keyword 'weight loss' as it is very competitive and has a high search volume. To bring in more traffic, you can use keywords in your website such as 'diet plan for weight loss' or something like 'meal plan for extreme weight loss'. These two suggested keywords are less competitive in comparison to 'weight loss'. One of the excellent keyword research tools is Keyword Revealer.

'Monthly volume' represents the search volume in your market, and volume trends give us an idea about the keyword search volume over the past 12 months. From the keywords suggested, we find that the 'weight loss tea' is less competitive when compared to 'quick weight loss' or 'weight loss' itself. Difficulty score is given out of 100, indicating how difficult it is for a website to appear on the first page of Google search results. You can find more details explaining the difficulty score if you click on the 'difficulty' tab for a chosen keyword.

---

[3] http://illuminationconsulting.com/7-statistics-and-facts-that-show-the-significanceof-seo/ (accessed on 12 December 2019).

If you are a beginner, you must prefer less difficult keywords, usually under 30. Next is the 'keyword search volume', which gives us an idea about the search volume in the past year in a graphical manner. You may wish to target keywords whose volume is increasing over time to ensure you are selling products whose demand is growing with time as high tide raises all ships. Google Trends depict the popularity of the keyword over a stipulated time.

The tool also shows the top 10 results for the keyword and gives various analytical insights for each of them, which we will discuss in this section. One important metric is 'domain authority' of a website which depicts the reputation, credibility and trust which users have in the website.

It is based on factors such as backlinks, how old the website is and the amount of traffic on the website. Therefore, a higher domain authority means a better ranking in the search engine results page. If the average domain authority is 89 out of 100, then it means that it is a very tough job to rank your website higher with 'weight loss' keyword. It means that you need to find a long-tail keyword which may have lesser volume but also less competition.

Typically, you can target keywords with 500 or less search volume, as keywords with more volume will have higher competition invariably. You must target keywords which have at least a few websites with a low domain authority (under 30) in top 10 results.

The next metric to look at is whether on-page optimization has been done for the keyword in the top 10 sites. This is reflected in the metrics URL, title, description and H1. If most sites have used proper meta tags, then there is limited opportunity to trump them by doing on-page optimization.

The above metrics give us an idea about how difficult it is to appear on the first page of the search engine results.

I would recommend that you choose keywords which have difficulty score lower than 30, the search volume of around 500 per month, an increasing volume trend, low domain authority of at least few sites in top 10 and low on-page optimization of at least few sites among the top 10.

Another metrics is accelerated mobile page (AMP). Search engines give preference to AMP sites, as they load immediately and hence user experience is better. Since the majority of the traffic to your site will be from smartphones, AMP will boost your traffic and reduce bounce rate. However, AMP can also mitigate user experience as it has many constraints in the usage of image and programming language.

Another strategy you can use to identify keywords is to use focal keywords along with the primary keywords and secondary keywords to rank the sites higher. To comprehend this, let's consider an example. 'President of the USA' could be a focal keyword, and 'POTUS' or 'White House' can be a primary keyword. The secondary keyword can be Donald Trump and Bill Clinton. With a proper content structured along these keywords, your page will be able to build the meaning or concept and hence will do better in semantic search. As technology is advancing, algorithms are becoming smarter, and search results are driven more by concept rather than keyword stuffing.

Google introduced latent semantic indexing (LSI), which picks up the content keywords used on your page and discards articles, prepositions, conjunctions, common verbs and pronouns. LSI is an indexing and retrieval method which identifies the semantics or meaning of the page by identifying relationships between the terms contained in an unstructured collection of text. You need not even mention the entire keyword in order, as LSI can correlate different words used in the page and stitch them together into a coherent meaning or concept. It is a smart idea to use synonyms instead of repeating the words and give both internal and external links to build the semantics of the page further. For example, 'plant' has two meanings: one is a shrub, and the other one is a factory. It is a good idea to use the plant as well as a shrub in your article as then search engine knows you are talking about vegetation.

Optimize Your Content to a Great Extent

After identifying the right keywords, you need to do on-page optimization using the techniques discussed here.

- First, the structure of your article should be highly ordered, meaning that it should contain a reasonable number of headings, subheadings and lists. This increases the readability, as your content gets divided into chunks of sections dedicated to addressing each issue. You can give them header tags such as H1 and H2. Typically, the focal keyword should appear in the title, and the title should be given the H1 tag. Subheadings can contain primary or secondary keywords and be given an H2 tag.

- Second, try to develop content which could answer some of the rudimentary questions regarding the keywords searched (preferably as early in the content as possible), thereby making it easily visible to the crawler. Easy visibility means better ranking.

- Third, tags are essential. Add tags wherever possible. Experienced affiliates use it in illustrations such as flowcharts and tables also. Videos and images should also be tagged with keywords. These tags are generally words or phrases which describe the content your website caters to.

- Fourth, make sure that the domain name of your website is easily discoverable by keeping it simple and memorable. Create a meaningful as well as a readable URL for the article; do not use default URL with parameters and question marks. As we know, the better readability, the higher the rank.

- Fifth, ensure that your articles are about 2,500 words each, as search engines prefer long-form articles since they are in-depth and well researched.[4] The bar diagram in Figure 9.1 shows that the blog articles which are longer have greater chances of ranking high in Google than shorter blog articles.

---

[4] https://www.webfx.com/blog/marketing/10-stats-you-need-to-know-about-seo/ (accessed on 12 December 2019).

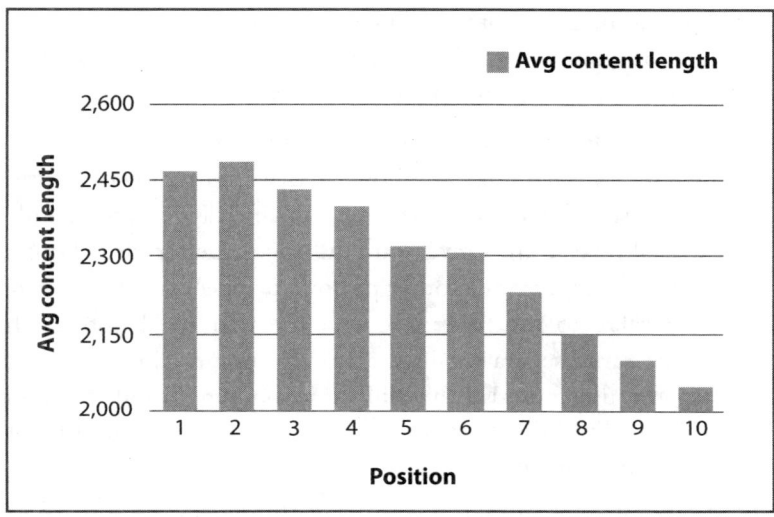

Figure 9.1: Average Word Length of the Top 10 Articles in Google

Source: https://cdnwp.mobidea.com/academy/wpcontent/uploads/ 2016/10/conten t-lenght-seo.jpg (accessed on 12 December 2019).

Add As Many Links As Possible

Yeah, you read it right! These are not just your affiliate links which we are referring to here. Links are one of the most important ranking factors in the Google algorithm, and it is indeed an advantage if you have more and more links in your posts rather than just your affiliate links.

What are these links?

Links are those which give reference to some other posts either in the same blog website or another site. There are two types of links which we will be discussing: internal and external. Adding them allows users to find related content and thus enhances the user experience.

- **Internal links:** These are the links in your post that lead the user somewhere in your website. Internal links are mainly used to provide supplementary information or a related study which could give a sharper understanding to the user, thereby building your website's reputation.

The advantage of internal links is that it keeps your user engaged in your website itself, thereby reducing the bounce rate and increasing the time spent on your site.

- **External links (also known as backlinks):** As the name suggests, external links are those links which redirect the user to a website which is outside your domain. It is good to include external links as they give your audience a better idea about a related concept from another person's perspective, thus adding more value to the readers so that the user need not search for the same separately in the search engine. This helps not only the user but also the affiliate in building a link with an established website, contributing to a more dependable content from your blog post.

Simple thumb rule to follow is to have 10 links on each page; of which, seven must be internal links and three external links. Every time you add a new page on your website, you must go back to old pages and link them to the new page. It will boost the link juice and SEO power of the new page.

Optimizing the Website for Mobile Users

Around 50 per cent of Internet traffic comes from mobile devices, and an average user spends up to 3 hours a day on mobile devices.[5] No one wants to laze around a sluggish website. So it's vital to make your website load fast so that the bounce rate is kept low (remember that the bounce rate is low for a high-speed website).

Deducing the areas to optimize for fast speed may feel quite technical for an affiliate like you. Don't worry; there are many tools to diagnose these technicalities. PageSpeed Insights, powered by Google, is specifically designed for diagnosing the health of your website across mobile as well as desktop platforms.

The numerical score represents the performance of the website. The score range of 0–49 means that the performance is slow and is

---

[5] https://ahrefs.com/blog/search-traffic-study/ (accessed on 12 December 2019).

denoted by red, 50–89 means that the performance is average and is represented by orange, and 90–100 means that the performance is fast and is characterized by green. You can do the diagnosis for your website too. As an affiliate, you must take care of all these fundamental technicalities before you start marketing. After diagnosis, you can take help from web developers, or you can roll up the sleeves and optimize it yourself.

Get Backlinks

When other sites link to your website, it is like a third-party endorsement, which builds the reputation of your domain. A study by Ahrefs suggests that around 91 per cent of the web pages don't get organic traffic mainly because of the lack of backlinks in their web pages. This indicates how vital it is to enrich your content with backlinks.[6]

To get backlinks, you can do guest posting, participate in forums and question–answer sites such as Quora, submit articles in syndicate sites, submit your web page in directories, get listed in classified sites, etc. Cross-posting on social media will also give backlinks.

You can use tools like Google Analytics and Google Search Console to learn about the SEO performance of your website. This way, you will know whether the tactics you implemented to improve SEO worked or not.

So in this chapter, we have seen what SEO is, how it can be leveraged to the fullest from an affiliate's point of view and the nuances in the same.

---

[6] Ibid.

CHAPTER 10

ADVANCED PRACTICES IN AFFILIATE MARKETING

Having discussed the basics of affiliate marketing, we will now acquaint ourselves with some of the advanced practices in affiliate marketing which will make your profits soar through the roof!

AFFILIATE MARKETING STRATEGIES THROUGH EMAILS

With 3.9 billion active email users, email is a popular tool in the affiliate marketer's arsenal.[1] The main agenda of email marketing is to cater to potential customers by nurturing relations with them. Assume that 1,000 people have accessed your affiliate website, but unfortunately, only 10 per cent of them are interested in the product. An email list generally consists of the visitors who are impressed with your content and would love to read more of it. So if you have an email subscriber list with just 30 per cent of the visitors who accessed your website, then you're still catering to a broader audience who could be potential buyers in the future, if not now.

Now, the question is: How to add these potential buyers to an email list? Well, you can't force them to get added. One of the techniques followed by affiliates is to have a pop-up which appears after 30–50 per cent of the scroll or on exit, appealing the readers to subscribe to the website.

---

[1] https://www.radicati.com/wp/wp-content/uploads/2018/12/Email-Statistics-Report-2019-2023-Executive-Summary.pdf (accessed on 16 December 2019).

But wait. Is it that simple? Definitely not! The users need an incentive, or an opt-in offer if you want many people to subscribe to your content. This works in multiple ways such as offering them an e-book related to the product or service you're promoting or a coupon which avails discount on specific products. What value you provide to the customer matters the most. Apart from this, every other strategy you follow in email marketing is the same, ranging from maintaining exclusivity to producing top-notch content so that your mail is not straight away driven into the 'spam' folder.

One crucial aspect you have to consider as an affiliate marketer is the frequency at which you send out emails. A lot of users are annoyed when you send out emails every day or for that matter more than twice in a week. So it's vital to space your emails in such a way that the user indeed finds value for time invested in your emails. Some experienced marketers even suggest the use of multiple lists, just to segregate the people based on their interests. There are many email software such as Mailchimp, AWeber and GMass, which can automate your emails with autoresponders.

Like I mentioned in previous chapters, some affiliate programmes restrict you from using affiliate links in emails. So here are some smart ways to tackle this problem.

- **Truncate your content:** You can share some part of your article in the mail. This way, you will be able to use email marketing without violating any regulations. Please make sure that there is no affiliate link in the shared part of the article, which will make the whole process of truncating the feed futile.
- **Plug-ins:** If you want the whole article in the email, you can use a plug-in which removes all the affiliate links from the content.

Paid Advertising for Affiliate Marketing

In simple language, paid advertising is where you pay for your affiliate product's advertisements to be shown. You decide when and where an ad appears on the Internet.

Paid ads can be an effective way to promote your affiliate products because:

- People start seeing your advertising as soon as you launch your campaigns, so the results are immediate (conversions might start flowing in immediately).
- You can tailor the targeting to meet your needs, which means that you can target a wide audience at once or just particular demographics/interest groups (in case of social media platforms).
- Various monitoring systems can be used to evaluate the promotional activities (you know exactly how much you spend on what kind of content and how much profit it brings).
- You have full control over how, where and when you promote your product.

However, there are a few drawbacks to consider:

- Your scope is restricted by the budget. If you have only $20 to spend on advertisements per day, you'll only be able to reach as many people as the $20 would allow.
- For beginners, it can be expensive since finding the right targeting takes time.
- Managing a large number of promotional campaigns can be exhausting.
- It necessitates financial commitment as well as understanding the fundamentals of affiliate marketing.

There are three payment options.

- **CPC:** You pay each time someone clicks on your ad. Assume you spend $0.03 per visit, and each of the products you sell on your website costs $5. You would pay $1.8 for ads if 60 people visit your website. If 10 people buy your stuff, you'll make $50. When you exclude the expense of ads from your revenue, you're left with a surplus of $48.20.
- **CPM:-** You'll be charged for every 1,000 views your ad receives. As an example, if your ad is seen 2,000 times and your

CPM is $1, you would pay $2. This payoff model is commonly used for generating awareness.

Flat rate: This can be used when you plan to buy an ad spot for a fixed price and for a certain period of time. If your ad spot costs $50 a day and you rent it for 7 days, you'll pay $350. You could get 5 sales for $5 each day, but that won't cover the cost of the ad spot. However, you could get 30 ($300) sales the next day, making up for any previous losses. Following are the ways in which you can use paid ads for affiliate marketing.

- **Google AdWords:** You can create an account and pay to display your ads on the top of the search results list, so if a user enters a keyword related to your website, Google will suggest your website.

- You can pay to have your ads displayed on social media platforms such as Instagram and Facebook, so that when a user clicks on your ad, they are directed to your website/landing page.

TYPES OF CONTENT: NOT JUST REVIEWS!

Many affiliates, especially beginners, believe that a blog can only contain reviews of affiliate products.[2] This is a misconception as there are a lot of means through which affiliates can engage the users and convince them to buy from their link.

- **Comparison content:** The affiliate does a comparative analysis of two or more rival products so that the reader gets an idea about the pros and cons of each product and can make a decision.

- **Case study posts:** It gives an in-depth analysis of the history of the product. These posts are generally aimed at providing the user with an appreciation of how the product has become,

---

[2] https://bloggingx.com/advanced-affiliate-marketing/#types-of-affiliate-blog-posts (accessed on 16 December 2019).

what it is and innuendo of how knowledgeable you are as a marketer, rather than pushing the reader to buy the product. For example, a case study can elaborate on Apple iPhone design from the first generation to the latest models.

- **Budget-based content:** Many users look for products under a specific budget. You can promote a product with the perspective of how it is one of the best under a particular price category, for example, a marketer promoting brand X's sunglasses with the blog title as 'Best Shades under ₹1,200'.

- **Tutorial-based content:** This type of content is intended to educate the readers with a specific skill or a task in general. The readers who go through these articles are mostly new to the field you are promoting. So you are bestowed with an added responsibility of guiding your readers authentically. Tutorial posts are one of the best ways to establish yourself as an authority in a field.

SOCIAL MEDIA AUTOMATION

By posting regularly on social media, you can reinforce your products and services. You can use tools to automate your posts across social media, thereby increasing your presence online. Some standard tools are Buffer and Hootsuite.

How does content automation work?

These tools queue your content for a stipulated time of your choice. Your role is to upload the content (tailor-made for different platforms is preferred) all at once via these tools and fix the date and time when you would ideally want to post it on social media platforms. In this way, the manual work of posting content is reduced. Many experienced marketers upload a few articles at leisure and queue them up for the upcoming week. Not just scheduling posts, but these automation sites also provide you with some useful insights.

You can identify a fair number of insights such as post engagement, response time and mentions. For affiliate marketers, these insights provide acumen to follow different strategies to develop a fan base and give an understanding of what exactly transpired around their post (people's reaction). These social media management platforms provide affiliates with the ideal opportunity to optimize their content and draw actionable insights to scale themselves into a brand, without breaking a sweat.

Buffer is another tool which does the same with some additional features such as drafting posts.

A/B TESTING IN AFFILIATE MARKETING

A/B testing is a way of juxtaposing two different ideas or choices and coming to a conclusion as to which one is better. Let us take the example of a banner on your website. Suppose there are two banners which you could incorporate in your site, and you are facing a dilemma as to which one should be posted. To arrive at a decision, you need to show banner 'A' to some site visitors and banner 'B' to others and analyse the conversion rate in both the cases. This method is also known as 'split testing'. Remember that the banner should be shown until you feel that conclusive results have been derived from the test. A simple flow chart in Figure 10.1 shows how A/B testing works.

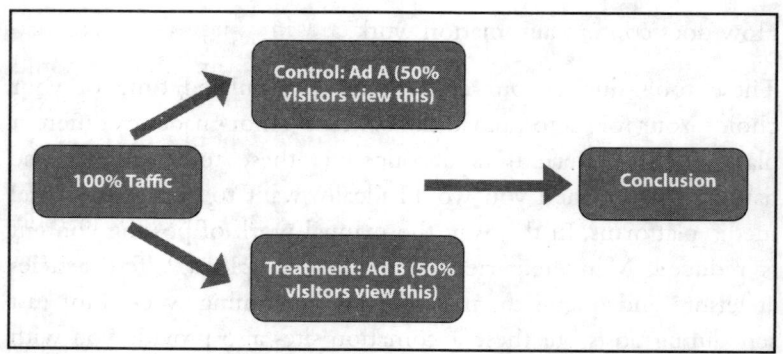

Figure 10.1: A simple Flow Chart of A/B Testing

The variable element in Figure 10.1 is the ad. It can be anything—ads, traffic sources, landing pages, titles, offers and prices. Control consists of the existing ad (Ad A), and treatment consists of the new ad which you wish to test (Ad B). A standard tool used to split the flow of traffic is Voluum. It uses traffic distribution artificial intelligence for the two paths if you have good enough traffic. Usually, the users' engagement is recorded and analysed through a statistical engine.

If you don't have significant traffic, then it's more than enough that you analyse it manually by observing the CTR and the conversion rate of different ads.

So why is A/B testing so necessary?

About 77 per cent of the companies run A/B testing in their websites, and 60 per cent of the Companies believe that A/B testing is vital to improving conversion rate.[3] A/B testing can be used to optimize smaller elements within a marketing campaign such as landing pages, ads, images, CTA, colours and layouts.

A/B testing allows affiliates to improve user experience on their website. Sometimes A/B testing acts as a reality check for some affiliates, thus making them realize that their way of thinking is not matching that of users. Refer to Figure 10.2 for stages in A/B testing.

LEVERAGING GOOGLE ALERTS FOR AFFILIATE PRODUCT NOTIFICATIONS

It is vital to stay ahead of the evolving trends in your product category. So how do you do this? You might think that an affiliate should go through a plethora of news articles daily to keep themselves updated in their niche. Well, that sounds like a lot of work.

Through Google Alerts, you could set up alerts for every affiliate product you promote and the major companies involved in their manufacture. You will receive alerts from Google if there is any

---

[3] https://www.inexhibit.com/case-studies/apple-iphone-history-of-a-design-revolution/ (accessed on 16 December 2019).

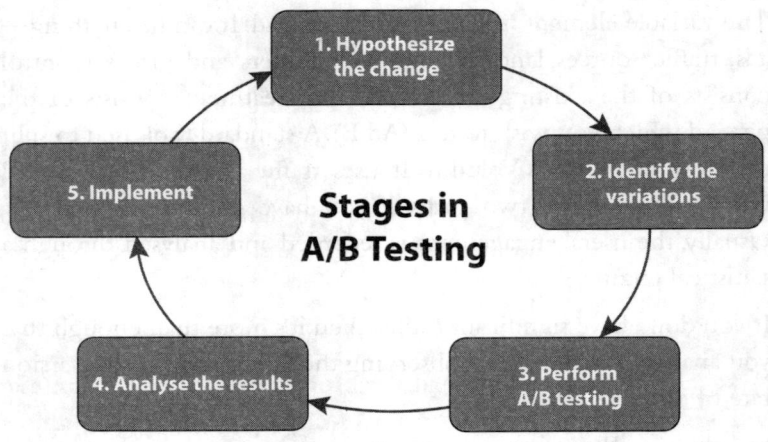

Figure 10.2: Stages in A/B Testing

news article, blogs, research or any latest updates concerning the keyword you had set up.

You might be wondering as to why there is a dire necessity for getting instant updates. The answer to this question is pretty simple: to stay ahead of the rest. Let us suppose a clothing brand 'X' which you used to promote is found out to be bogus or the consumer satisfaction is not up to the mark. With the aid of Google Alerts, you will be one of the first few to know about this, and you can instantly warn your readers/viewers not to fall into the trap of brand 'X'. Similarly, the other side of the coin could be that let's suppose that brand 'X' has launched a brand new jacket which is unique in terms of styling; you can promote it fast among your users and thereby make more money.

TOOLS FOR AFFILIATE LINK PLACEMENT

Crazy Egg and Clicktale are tools showing 'heat maps', which indicate places where visitors tend to click more often than others and how far they have scrolled down. This is visualized using the spectrum between warm and cold colours. The colour code gives us an idea about the magnitude of clicks on a particular position and the customer behaviour in a specific site.

For elucidation, let's consider the Crazy Egg tool. Rich features will allow you to know the exact behaviour of the users as they surf through your website. Features such as scroll map report indicate how much a user scrolls through your site. Confetti report shows the demographics, referrers and devices used to access the website.

So how do you get started with a tool like Crazy Egg?

A universal notion is to install a tracking code to your website as soon as you sign up for any tool like Crazy Egg. This establishes a connection between Crazy Egg and your website, thereby opening up a channel to collect and analyse data.

After installing a tracking script, you have to create 'snapshots', which are nothing but heat maps with all the relevant features according to your needs. For example, snapshots can have click map, scroll map and confetti report.

As an affiliate marketer, analysing a confetti report will tell you from where exactly traffic comes to your site, thereby allowing you to optimize for different traffic sources. An attractive feature in Crazy Egg is the Crazy Egg editor, which doesn't need a web developer to modify content in your website. This is a handy tool which allows you to change element styles, including font colour and size. Crazy egg also provides A/B testing for factors such as content placement, image and colour. A/B testing is a technique for determining statistically which of the two variants of any factor gets a better response from the market. The factors which can be tested can be landing pages, price, discounts, layout, colour, creative, etc.

PRODUCT LAUNCH JACKING IN AFFILIATE MARKET

It is a technique where affiliates across the globe take advantage of new products launched in the market by posting relevant content on them, which entices the audience to buy them. Marketers leverage this opportunity when there is a buzz around the product, and customers are interested to know more about the product.[4] It is always an advantage if you are one of the first marketers to post content related to new products. If you could post the content some weeks before the actual launch of the product, then you might earn better organic traffic in Google Search engine as well. Some of the related practices include distributing coupons, announcing massive discounts (early bird purchases) and giving additional perks such as providing earphones for free when you're promoting smartphones. Certain thumb rules for a successful product launch jacking strategy are as follows:

- **Identifying the sites to select the newly launched products:** Product launch jacking is about introducing the latest products when the customers are still immersed in the thrill and excitement of getting to know about a new product. Some of the recommended websites for learning these newly launched products are muncheye.com, warriorplus.com and JVZoo.
- **Positioning your content by leveraging SEO:** Many marketers are waiting to market newly launched products. So there is an innate necessity to leverage SEO to optimize your presence online, as we discussed in the previous chapter.

Product launch jacking is similar to optimizing your content with the help of SEO except for the added constraint of timing, jacking up incentives, lucrative discounts and offers. They create urgency by using lines such as 'Limited seating. Please reserve your spot'.

Some of the ways by which you can optimize product launch jacking are by incorporating social bookmarks, videos and article submissions.

HEADLINE ANALYSER

Despite writing a high-quality blog or posting an informative video, unless users click on your link or ad, they wouldn't be able to read your content. To write a catchy headline, experienced affiliates

---

[4] https://www.invespcro.com/blog/the-state-of-ab-testing/ (accessed on 17 December 2019).

take the aid of tools such as CoSchedule's Headline Analyzer. After signing up on CoSchedule, you just need to enter the title you feel apt for the blog post, and then CoSchedule analyses and flashes results depending on the type of words used in the headline.[5]

The score is awarded based on four metrics, which are discussed further:

- Common words are those words which contribute to the basic structure of the headline. Experts suggest that common words make up around 20–30 per cent of the headlines only. 'To', 'and', 'can', etc., come under this category.

- Uncommon words are the less frequent words, which build up the substance of the headline, and are ideally preferred in the range of 10–20 per cent to concoct a traffic generating headline.

- Emotional words are those which instigate an emotion within the reader. For example, 'comfortable' could be used in a blog where you are promoting products which make the customer's life easy. Emotional words make up 10–15 per cent of good headlines.

- Power words are those which drive the attention of the reader and motivate them to click on your blog. These words are the most persuasive ones in terms of making the visitor click on your site. At least one power phrase or word is needed for a good headline. Examples include 'best', 'perfect' and 'instant'.

So in this chapter, we have gained an understanding of advanced practices followed by affiliates across the world. As your affiliate marketing grows, you need to follow the latest trends, reduce manual work and leverage tools to make profits.

---

[5] https://help.coschedule.com/hc/en-us/articles/215563057-Working-with-the-Headline-Analyzer (accessed on 18 December 2019).

CHAPTER 11

SUPPLEMENTARY WISDOM IN AFFILIATE MARKETING

In this chapter, we will discuss Google AdSense and how affiliates leverage the same crypto affiliate programmes, the significance of native ads in affiliate marketing and some of the guidelines one must follow as an affiliate as per the Federal Trade Commission (FTC).

GOOGLE ADSENSE

AdSense is an ad product from Google which displays ads based on the content's context in your blog. It is one of the go-to modes of making money through advertising if you're a blogger. The best part is that as a blogger, you get paid whenever the user clicks the ad on your blog site (in some cases, if the user just sees!). The only hurdle is to get an approved AdSense account. You can integrate with AdSense by either using WordPress plug-ins or by manually inserting the code.[1] Refer to Figure 11.1 to get an overview of how AdSense works.

The best part of AdSense is that you need not create a new account for every site, like other ad networks, when you have multiple sites. Once you get an approved AdSense account, you can add ads in your sites which comply with the 'Terms of Service' of Google. Even if you are managing sites with similar niches, AdSense gives

---

[1] https://www.shoutmeloud.com/AdSense-guide (accessed on 20 December 2019).

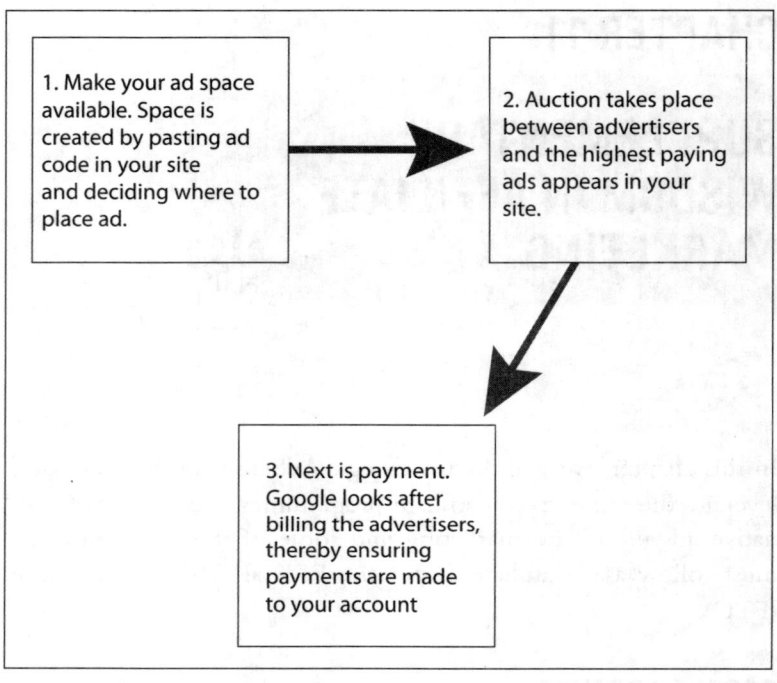

Figure 11.1: How AdSense Works

you the approval to append the ad code in your multiple sites, provided that the content is original and unique in some aspect. AdSense gives you the passive recurring flow of income, which supplements affiliate income. Getting an approved AdSense account signifies your blog site's credibility, adding a feather in your cap as an affiliate.

Comparison between Adsense and Affiliate Marketing

One of AdSense's most significant drawbacks is the cumbersome process involved in setting up an approved account. The protocols to be followed are manifold, and one should be updated about them now and then. But on the other hand, setting up an account in an affiliate network is an easy process. Also, since Google manages

AdSense, affiliates find it better to go with AdSense rather than opt for other small networks; that is, the affiliates have to rely solely on AdSense and don't have a choice. AdSense programme policies are to be referred to regularly if you own an AdSense account.

So is affiliate marketing better than AdSense? Well, yes, to an extent! But if you want to be an efficient affiliate marketer, you have to consider establishing a synergy between AdSense and affiliate marketing.

ESTABLISHING THE SYNERGY

And as we have discussed in earlier chapters, not all the blog posts you publish will roll out profits, especially if you create content for all the three stages of the funnel as discussed earlier (top, middle and bottom). Predominantly, affiliates drop their links at the BOFU posts. So is monetization possible in the upper stages of the funnel? Certainly yes, and that's where Google AdSense comes into play. AdSense works fine even on those web pages where you have not placed affiliate links owing to your content strategy. Instead of null profit, you might earn some money if the user clicks on the ad.

Summing it up, you can follow AdSense and affiliate banners in the right combination so that you monetize all the blog pages. Rely more on AdSense when there isn't scope for affiliate links, and vice versa when you believe that there is greater scope for promoting affiliate links.

CRYPTOCURRENCY AFFILIATE PROGRAMMES

Who hasn't heard about Bitcoin, which is a cryptocurrency? A cryptocurrency is a decentralized digital currency without a central bank or single administrator sent from user to user on the peer-to-peer Bitcoin network without the need for intermediaries. In simple words, cryptocurrency is digital money wherein transactions are secured through cryptography. Transactions are recorded in a blockchain, which is a public distributed ledger.[2]

So should an affiliate promote Bitcoins?

Well, certainly yes! You could do that within the geographical boundary, which recognizes cryptocurrency as a legitimate digital currency mode. The USA, European Union and many other countries recognize cryptocurrency as a legitimate means to carry out trade. A report by Leftronic states that Bitcoin's market capitalization, one of the most popular cryptocurrencies, is a mammoth $144.96 billion.[3] Therefore, there is no shortage of opportunities as a 'crypto affiliate'. However, watch your step before promoting cryptocurrency; familiarize yourself with different regulations in different countries.

What decides the price of Bitcoin, and should you deal in it?

Unlike other stock options, there is no balance sheet or financial statement to review before buying a Bitcoin. The Bitcoin price is determined by factors such as demand and supply, government regulations and the cost of producing a Bitcoin. So unlike stock options, determining the life and growth of Bitcoin is unpredictable. On the other hand, the Supreme Court's judgment favouring cryptocurrency is likely to spur cryptocurrency investment. So you need to be extra careful while dealing with it, considering the volatile nature of the currency. There was a sharp peak in the price in 2018, and it is attributed to the rise in Bitcoins' popularity, and then there was a steep decrease in 2019 which was because of the legal restrictions imposed in many countries after that.

You can make some good money by promoting some of the in-demand cryptocurrencies across the world. Affiliates must keep in mind that cryptocurrencies' legality may not be the same forever.

[2] https://support.google.com/AdSense/answer/48182utm_source=aso&utm_medium=link&u tm_campaign=ww-ww-et-asfe_&gsessionid=6j8PVi4fvPrGzuk7-kh1RQ (accessed on 21 December 2019).

[3] https://www.jbs.cam.ac.uk/fileadmin/user_upload/research/centres/alternative-finance/downloads/2017-global-cryptocurrency-benchmarking-study.pdf (accessed on 21 December 2019).

A crypto affiliate pretty much works the same way as that of the rest of the affiliate products. You need to sign up for the respective Bitcoin programmes which you prefer to promote. And you receive a commission for every registration made on the cryptocurrency website through your affiliate link (which will be uniquely generated once you sign up).

But the only varying factor in the case of crypto affiliate programmes is that you are deemed either a one-time referral bonus (once the user registers in the cryptocurrency website) or lifetime passive income (you earn a commission for every transaction made by the user through that particular cryptocurrency). Sometimes, you have the option of getting your commission paid in the form of Bitcoins, provided your country's jurisdiction entertains the same. Some of the standard affiliate programmes are listed below.[4]

- **CEX.IO affiliate programme:** You get paid a 30 per cent commission for all the transactions. Due to the high reputation enjoyed by this programme, a lot of affiliates prefer it.

- **Coinbase referral programme:** You'll be paid $10 for each referral which buys or sells at least $100 or more within 180 days of registration. The best part is that the person you refer also receives $10, thus making Coinbase one of the sought-after crypto affiliate programmes across the world.

- **LocalBitcoins affiliate programme:** You earn 20 per cent each for referring a buyer or a seller.

- **Bitbond affiliate programme:** You can earn up to 50 per cent commission, that is, 20 per cent commission for every borrower you refer to Bitbond and 30 per cent commission for every lender you refer.[5]

---

[4] https://leftronic.com/cryptocurrency-statistics/ (accessed on 21 December 2019).
[5] https://makeawebsitehub.com/best-bitcoin-affiliate-programs/ (accessed on 23 December 2019).

NATIVE ADS IN AFFILIATE MARKETING

Native advertisements, as the name suggests, are native to a website, which means that native ads just blend with the content, and the visitor, in most cases, is oblivious of the fact that it was an ad indeed because these ads don't look like ads in the first place.

In many of the native ads, you might find an appealing factor which leads to conversion. An example of an appealing factor is 'How to make money', and many people will click out of curiosity to make money! In some ads, you might recognize emotions being the appealing factor, which entices the user to click on the native ad.

Initially, you have to sign up on any native ad source like MGID or Taboola and create an account. You will often be asked to deposit some funds depending on the native ad platform, and you need to set up your campaign specifying what you are looking to promote (content or the product), who your target audience is, their preferred language, geographical location, etc. Be ready with some investment at your disposal.

Native ads ensure that your campaign is unique in comparison to fellow marketers. Because ads blend with content, they result in a unique marketing campaign. When a customer sees your ad at the bottom of some other site, they will click through the ad if they are genuinely interested in the content. This way, you have just found out a method which can promote your content further.

Native ad sources ensure that your ads are published on various other sites with content on similar lines. So although native ads cost some money, the bottom line is that if an appropriate strategy is deployed, it can do wonders for you as an affiliate marketer. As large as 67.2 per cent tend towards clicking sponsored articles (native ads basically) compared to banner ads.[6] Leveraging native ads could bring in significant traffic to your site from other websites.

---

[6] https://www.charlesngo.com/beginners-guide-native-advertising-for-affiliate-marketing/ (accessed on 23 December 2019).

Significance of Native Ads in Affiliate Marketing

You can also deploy native ads concept in your website. Often blog visitors tend to utterly ignore the ad (also known as banner blindness) and turn down various advertising techniques per se. So as an affiliate marketer, it becomes a challenging task to promote advertisements in your post. But native ads can save your day as these ads just blend in and do not appear like an ad, and hence users are more likely to click on such links than banners on your website.

Figure 11.2 shows a glimpse of native ads CTRs by product category. As you can see, pets and food top the charts when it

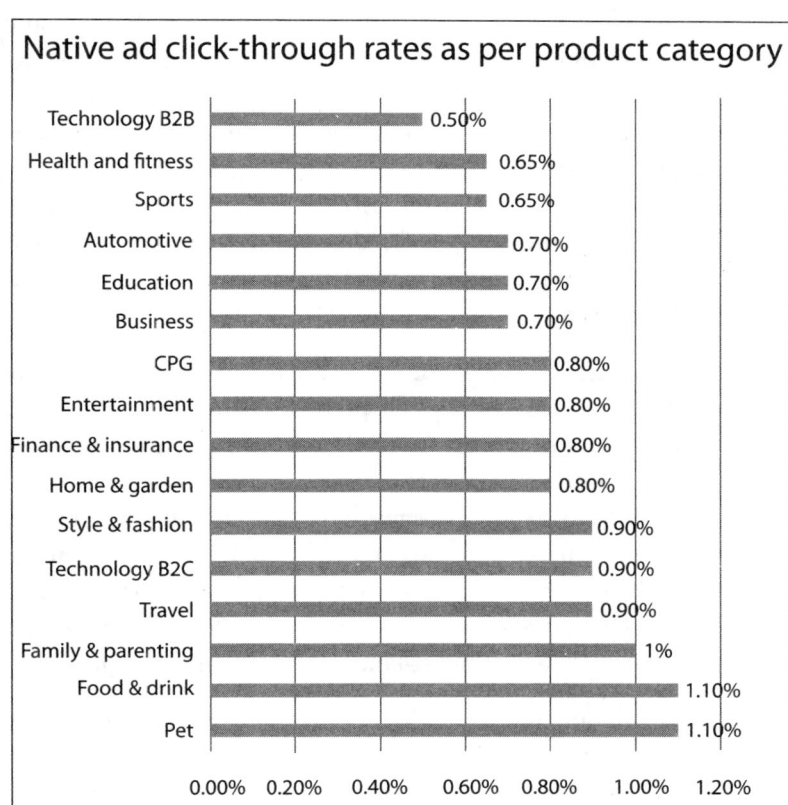

Figure 11.2: Native Ad CTRs as per Product Category

Source: https://www.adweek.com/wpcontent/uploads/2017/04/JornerGuestPostNativeAdvertis ing.png (accessed on 24 December 2019).

comes to CTR. CTR is 1.1 per cent for pets and food. You might find that the CTRs are a bit less, but I must tell you that this CTR is much higher than regular banner ads, which have an average CTR of 0.3 per cent only. Most importantly, these visitors are genuinely interested in the content being advertised through the native ad.

MISTAKES TO AVOID AS AN AFFILIATE MARKETER

We will take a glance at some mistakes you ought to avoid if you want to fly high as an affiliate marketer.

1. One of the major mistakes is 'affiliates running amok in pursuit of making money'. Some of the affiliates become aggressive marketers by coercing the user to 'buy' the product at any cost. Now, you have to understand the fine line between affiliate marketing and sales. You are just guiding the users towards making a choice, and in the process, the commission can be perceived as remuneration for the service you have provided. Living up to this attitude is what makes some of the affiliates stand out in the industry.

2. Diversifying is good, but you can't be limitless. If you recollect, in the earlier chapter, I mentioned how not to rely on just one affiliate network; instead, sign up for multiple accounts to mitigate risks and ensure a steady flow of income. Some affiliates become overzealous and end up in a tangle with many affiliate accounts and are unable to manage either of them. So before signing up for a new affiliate network, analyse whether you would be able to handle all the networks simultaneously with utmost efficiency and time management.

3. Tracking your affiliate links is essential, especially if you're promoting multiple products on different pages across your website. Many affiliates tend to forget this and end up perplexed about the link through which the sale happened in the first place. To track your link, go to the settings section in your affiliate account and ensure that you track all the links.

4. Newbie affiliate marketers do not entirely leverage comparison marketing. What I mean is that instead of mainstream content of reviewing a product, you need to compare a set of best performers in the market (types of content were discussed in Chapter 10). Two main objectives are satisfied by comparison marketing. First, you have catered to the visitors' interest by promoting comparison content, which gives them fine details about how one aces over the other on different criteria. Second, if you are bestowing on the visitors to choose whichever product they want, you can undoubtedly drop affiliate links for each product individually. By tracking the purchases made through the links, you would get an idea of the product which performs well, and then you can market that particular product more aggressively.

5. Being a jack of all trades and master of none doesn't work well in affiliate marketing. You cannot put yourself into promoting any and every niche. Managing too many niches is not easy. You may also realize that you can make more money by consolidating your efforts in one niche rather than fragmenting it over too many niches.

ENDORSEMENT GUIDELINES

This section gives you an idea about the guidelines set up by the FTC for affiliate marketing.

Now, let's take a brief overview of some of the critical factors to be kept in mind as affiliates.[7]

There should be a clear and conspicuous disclosure which informs the visitors that you as an affiliate will get paid a specific commission for purchases which take place by clicking on your link. Disclosures should be placed in those positions where the visitor could easily find them at the first go, maybe near the product recommendation

---

[7] https://www.ftc.gov/tips-advice/business-center/guidance/ftcs-endorsement-guides-what-people-are-asking#affiliateornetwork (accessed on 24 December 2019).

itself. Putting them after the entire product review or somewhere camouflaged behind a hyperlink won't work. Ideally, FTC recommends you to place the disclosure at the beginning of the article itself. For example, you can have a hyperlink with relevant anchor text, which on clicking leads to the affiliate disclosure page.

Sometimes you will see the disclosure being given in the form of a hyperlink at the top of the blog post. Remember that all the above regulations are mandated across the USA only, but most countries impose regulations on similar lines.

You are supposed to clearly disclose if you are getting any kind of compensation. Apart from the direct affiliate commission, compensation can be in many forms:

1. Cash payments
2. Sample or demo products
3. Store credits in your account
4. Gifts from the advertiser
5. Special discounts
6. Free giveaway items
7. Gift cards
8. Any other kind of 'favour'

Best Practices to Disclose Your Affiliate Links

The following are the best practices to disclose your affiliate links:

1. Directly place the entire disclosure at a place on your website where it is clearly visible (e.g., the top of the page).
2. If you don't want to leave the complete disclosure on the page, you can leave a link to the disclosure page.
3. It is advised to avoid putting your affiliate disclosure statement below the fold of a website.

4. Track the CTR of your affiliate disclosure link to check if the link is clearly visible to the visitors.

5. The FTC's rules apply to every online format, including articles, blog posts, social media posts, video content, podcasts, webinars, infographics and illustrations. For platforms like Twitter, where character limit is an issue, you can use sponsored text like #ad or #sponsored.

6. The FTC states that banner ads do not need to be disclosed, as people can understand the intent. However, posting a banner on the page with affiliate links doesn't exempt you from posting a disclosure, whether or not the banner relates to the article's content.

7. Do mention that the commission is paid entirely by the company, and your audience won't have to pay anything extra.

8. Add a short affiliate disclosure text widget on the sidebar, and make it fixed. This will make your users constantly aware of it.[8]

How to Use Disclosure in Your Favour?

Whether you like it or not, you have to disclose affiliate links. Now, disclosing affiliate links can make your audience a bit sceptical about your recommendation, which is natural on their part. It is your job to convince your audience that you are recommending the best product based on your experience and would have recommended it even if you weren't getting a commission.

The first thing is that you need to be confident about your recommendation. Claim that you use affiliate links openly and confidently.

Users always respect transparency. The use of humour to disclose the affiliate statement is also an excellent way to address your

---

[8] https://blog.aweber.com/affiliate-marketing/every-affiliate-marketer-needs-know-ftc-disclosure-guidelines.htm (accessed on 15 May 2020); https://nomnompaleo.com// (accessed on 15 May 2020).

audience. For example, Chris Brogan says, 'If you buy this from me, I get some beer money (not enough for a pony)'.

Another great way is to provide all the options that your audience can use to reach the product (the ones you earn nothing from also). This shows that you care for your audience more than you care about your commission.

Wondering if this technique works?

In an experiment that was conducted, it was found that 76 per cent chose the affiliate link, and only 24 per cent chose the non-affiliate link.

So the bottom line is that always recommend the product that will genuinely help your audience and be open about the genuine efforts you had put in your work and how it will generate revenue for you.

CHAPTER 12

LET'S TALK INFLUENCER MARKETING

Having discussed various aspects of affiliate marketing, it is time to move to another common means of making money online: influencer marketing. If you are an expert in a particular field and enjoy fan following in social media, influencer marketing should be your best choice to make money online. In this chapter, we will be discussing what influencer marketing is and how it can benefit brands and the influencer and how to go about doing influencer marketing.

WHAT IS INFLUENCER MARKETING?

Influencer marketing is a technique which focuses on leveraging experts or individuals who have a strong appeal in social media platforms in a particular niche—be it fashion, food or travel. Brands get their products endorsed through influencers. These individuals have already established a reputation for themselves in a specific field and have loyal fans.

In influencer marketing, brands initiate a partnership with influencers to promote their products through the latter's social media handles. Influencer marketing industry was about $10 billion by 2020. For example, Linus Sebastian, a Canadian YouTuber, is quite famous in the computer hardware niche. Therefore, many companies approach him to promote their products through his explicit content. A similar example will be of GeekyRanjit, an Indian YouTuber who specializes in the technology field.

Through these 'Internet celebrities', brands can efficiently market their products to the masses through a credible medium. Most of these companies pay the influencers, apart from giving out the products for free. You may ask why these companies directly do not use the common marketing channels or approach celebrities to promote the products through ads.

Increasingly, users trust the recommendations by influencers over celebrities such as actors, musicians and sportspeople. The main reason is the user's lack of product knowledge, while the influencers are ingenious in their respective fields. The actors do not genuinely review the pros and cons of the product; instead, they just read out the 'script' given to them by the ad agency. For instance, an actor who promotes smartphones need not be well versed with the phone they are endorsing.

Also, actors seldom mention the 'cons' of the product they are promoting. In that case, the user doesn't get a complete idea of the product being talked about. In 2018, a study found that only 4 per cent of people trusted celebrity advertisements.[1] On the other hand, influencers' main strength is their fields' knowledge, coupled with a loyal fan following.

Influencers develop various content types such as honest product reviews, unboxing videos and comparison videos to promote the product. People are more likely to get allured towards purchasing a product on influencers' recommendations or any familiar person.

With many companies adopting influencer marketing, the budget for influencer marketing has increased by a whopping 65 per cent.[2] In Figure 12.1, we observe that 7 per cent of the companies are ready to invest over $1 million in influencer marketing, showing the confidence that marketers have in influencers.

---

[1] https://blog.hubspot.com/marketing/how-to-become-an-influencer-in10steps (accessed on 13 May 2020).

[2] https://www.instagram.com/p/B5JN5AGJtK7/?utm_source=ig_web_copy_link (accessed on 27 December 2019).

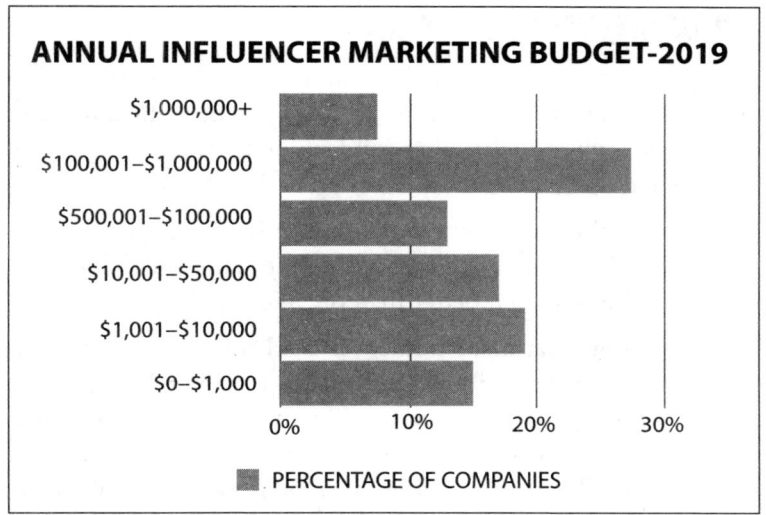

Figure 12.1: Annual Influencer Marketing Budget
Source: https://mediakix.com/influencermarketingresources/influencermarketingroi/ (accessed on 27 December 2019).

Influencer marketing is closely associated with social media marketing and content marketing, although they are not the same. You might be thinking that why don't brands invest in digital ads instead of influencers. The reason is simple: banner blindness. It is said that 86 per cent of consumers suffer from banner blindness.[3]

Customers these days tend to ignore digital ads or use ad-blocking technology to ensure that they are not interrupted. This has hugely affected digital ads with as large as 198 million active ad block users worldwide as of 2015.[4] About content marketing, some brands issue the content beforehand itself to the influencers. However, influencers prefer making their content, which has a distinct character and tonality.

---

[3] https://www.omnivirt.com/blog/prevent-banner-blindness/ (accessed on 13 May 2020).
[4] https://pagefair.com/blog/2015/ad-blocking-report/ (accessed on 27 December 2019).

RISE OF INFLUENCER MARKETING

The age-old strategy of brands running excessive and repetitive ads has backfired and has led to 'ad fatigue', where the ads are no longer productive. On the other hand, influencer marketing is cost-effective and doesn't irritate the consumer like the ads.

According to the data shown in Figure 12.2, influencer marketing is considered the fastest-growing online customer-acquisition method for brands, even better than organic search.

The two factors that make influencer marketing stand out in this regard are the authenticity it renders and the remedy it provides against 'ad fatigue' and 'banner blindness'. So brands prefer influencers who can bring in more conversions and engage with the audience. The best part from a brand's point of view is that many influencers market their products.

WHAT IS THE ROLE OF AN INFLUENCER IN EARNED MEDIA?

Earned media is the publicity 'earned' by the brand, unlike paid ads or banners. For example, a user sharing your product review

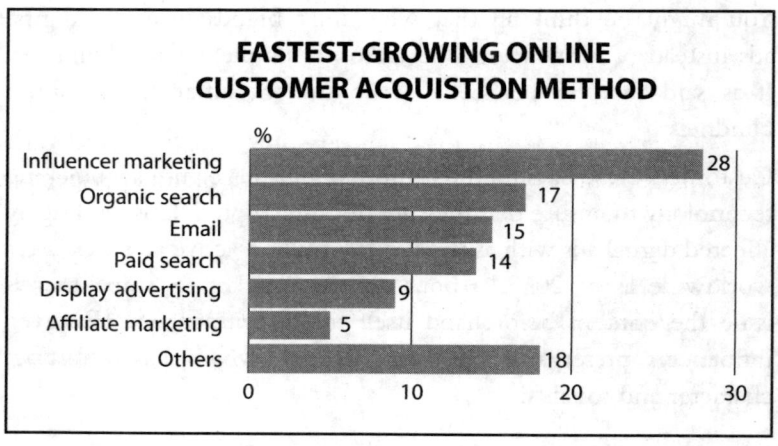

Figure 12.2: Fast-growing Customer Acquisition Methods

Source: https://influencermarketinghub.com/theriseofinfluencermarketing/#:~:text=Influencer (accessed on 10 July 2020).

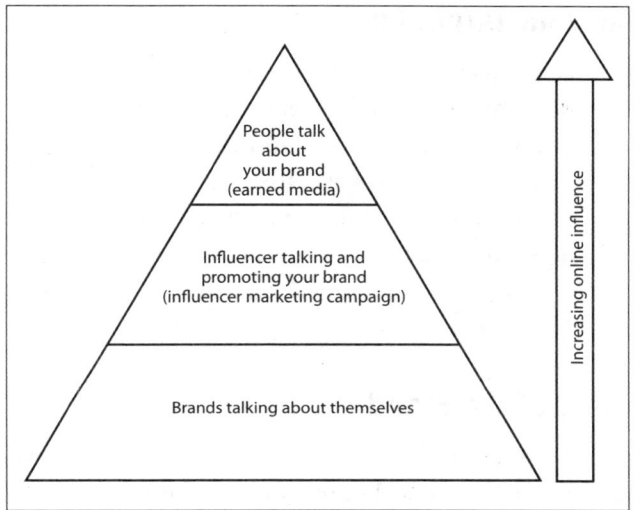

Figure 12.3: Pyramid Showing the Ranking of Earned Media in the Realm of Online Influence

on social media platforms is an example of earned media. As a brand, you did not pay the user to share the product review, but still, it happened, thereby 'earning' you some publicity. When a user shares a post, their friends and family members are influenced by the product. You may think that earned media is excellent, but what is the role of influencer marketing here? Influencers have earned followers' trust; hence, when they share content about the brand, followers engage in the conversation, and the brand earns this engagement. To illustrate the above from a brand's perspective, refer to the pyramid in Figure 12.3.[5]

GETTING STARTED WITH INFLUENCER MARKETING

It's essential to know what brands want if you want to succeed as an influencer. So let's take a look at the process of influencer marketing from the brand's point of view.

---

[5] https://static.jeffbullas.com/wp-ontent/uploads/2016/07/Infuencermarketinggoals.jpg (accessed on 27 December 2019).

Analyse Your Target Audience

Brands initiate a reconnaissance on who their target audience is for a particular product, as only then can they approach the right influencer to cater to the required audience. So if a brand comes to you for promotion, they have their goals figured out. As an influencer, you need to check if the audience they are looking to target matches your audience and decide accordingly. Accepting a bad deal will make you post something unusual, which will harm your image in the long run.

Objectives of the Brand

Brands can have different goals, such as leads, conversions, awareness or website traffic. Let us examine the essential objectives in detail.

1. **Visibility:** These brands are new to the market and digital platforms. They look to make a name for themselves on social networks, gain distinctness and impact users. Mainly, such campaigns' interesting metrics are the reach and engagement levels, which help to measure users' responses. Mostly, brands opt for exciting campaigns with a challenge for the audience to perform. Also, brands tend to favour several influencers over one macro influencer. For example, the ALS Ice Bucket Challenge was an online campaign in 2014 to raise awareness about the disease 'amyotrophic lateral sclerosis' (ALS) and raise funds. The campaign went viral and raised $115 million in just eight weeks. The challenge was to pour a bucket of ice water on yourself to support the campaign.

2. **Branding:** Brands use these campaigns to build a brand image or associate a particular quality or characteristic with the brand. Such campaigns help the brand in becoming recognizable and attaching attributes to it. In such campaigns, brands select influencers with very niche profiles and prefer to keep a long-term relationship with them to become brand ambassadors eventually.

For example, Puma appointed Virat Kohli as its brand ambassador to promote the brand. The Indian captain is known for his hard work and sheer dedication, and it complimented the brand's tagline 'Forever Faster'.[6]

3. **Positioning:** Every brand wants to be the first one that comes to the mind of the consumer. For this, consumers need to be updated with every new product that the brand releases and the detailed analysis. This is done by selecting the prominent influencers in your industry and sending them your product for a free trial. For example, OnePlus sent their flagship OnePlus 8 series to many influencers before the smartphone's official launch, with the condition that they will post their reviews.

4. **Traffic:** Brands often seek to generate traffic to their websites or social media profiles to increase visibility. This is achieved by campaigns across multiple platforms with giveaways, prizes, etc. Another method to achieve traffic is through mentions in Instagram stories which will directly lead the customer to the brand profile. Such traffic can be easily measured by the number of clicks on the URL.

5. **Conversion:** Conversion is a direct result of increased traffic and is one of the most common campaign objectives. An appropriate example would be giving influencers discount codes to share with their followers, which they then use upon checkout. In this campaign objective, the payment process must be user-friendly and optimal so that potential sales achieved through influencers are not lost.

6. **Brand loyalty:** This is also a crucial goal for many marketing campaigns. Most brands nudge people to post their experience with the brand's product for rewards.

You must note that these categories overlap with each other. As an influencer, you need to analyse the situation that the brands put forward and act accordingly.

---

[6] https://www.tapinfluence.com/blog-what-is-influencer-marketing/ (accessed on 27 December 2019).

How Do Brands Measure the Success of the Marketing Campaign?

By setting up efficient tracking methods, the brands can track the customer journey. Are customers aware of the brand, are they interested in the brand and do they prefer the brand over competitors? Some of the common factors they look for are to improve brand advocacy, the reach of newer audiences, engagement, leads and sales conversion. Knowing the brand's goal helps you prioritize your action as an influencer accordingly.

How to Choose the Right Influencers?

Now let's look at what matters the most to brands while looking for an influencer (refer to Figure 12.4).

Critical criteria are the match between the messaging of the influencer and the brand, the reach, the level of creativity, the engagement

Figure 12.4: Criteria for Selecting Influencers

Source: https://www.semrush.com/blog/viral-marketing-campaign-inspiration/ (accessed on 13 May 2020).

rate and the cost. Typically, brands will rate influencers on the above criteria. Sometimes, they assign weights to the above criteria depending on their objective, calculate weighted scores for different influencers on an Excel sheet and then select the influencer with the highest score. Understanding the brand's measures will help you set priorities in the journey of being an influencer.

How Do Brands Pay the Influencers?

Well, there are several different ways by which influencers can be paid.

CASH

Influencers usually charge according to per 1,000 views.

For example, if a YouTuber charges ₹3,000 per 1,000 views, then the amount you will pay is (₹3,000 × number of views/1,000) + some special rates for other handles.

FREE PRODUCTS AND DISCOUNT

This is one of the best ways to build a relationship. Often the brand gives them some free products because, in the future, when they use the brand, they will automatically promote it.

COMMISSION

This is a very straightforward way of doing business. With more sales, you get more commission. Hence, the commission is usually tied to sales.

How to Find Influencers?

Brands consider the best influencers who can execute the marketing campaign well. So let's see some of the ways through which brands identify influencers.

JUST SEARCH FOR THEM!

With the help of Google or any search engine, marketers visit the influencers' website to get to know them better and collect the contact details. But this is a time-taking process, so brands highly depend on online tools and influencer networks.

LEVERAGE THE TOOLS

Tools such as BuzzSumo, Klear and TweetDeck help the brands identify potential influencers. BuzzSumo, for instance, is extensively used by brands to identify content marketing influencers. A lot of filters accompanying this tool just make it one of the go-to tools for finding influencers.

INFLUENCER NETWORKS

Similar to an affiliate network, an influencer network is a platform where brands and influencers coexist. It helps brands discover influencers and vice versa. Even micro influencers with less than 100,000 followers can join these platforms. The major advantage of these networks is that they save a lot of time and provide ample choices for the brands and the influencers. In India, networks such as influencer.in, Plixxo and Mad Influence have been the front runners. Some other examples include influence.co, Activate and HelloSociety. Brands such as Himalaya, Axis Bank and Hike use 'influencer.in' to run their influencer marketing campaign.

Generally, influencers are divided into celebrity influencers, brand ambassadors already enticed by your brand and promoters who generate the buzz around the product through blogs and videos.

Why should an influencer work on a platform?

- **To build relationships:** These platforms allow influencers, especially beginners, to broaden their network and get assignments.
- **Chance to build credibility:** Once you manage to participate in a few influencer marketing campaigns for a platform,

you begin to create a portfolio of your work that other brands can see. In some ways, this works exponentially. The more successful you are at influencer marketing, the more brands take notice of you, and the chances of getting more work increase.

- **Creative freedom:** It can get overwhelming for influencers to negotiate for their artistic freedom directly. On the one hand, brands want you to review their products, but on the other hand, they feel that the content produced by you is theirs and not yours. The influencer platform helps by creating clear regulations and thus helps avoid conflict of interest.

Now, let's look at the factors every influencer should consider before selecting a platform.

What should an influencer look for in a platform?

- **Right balance between opportunities and competition:** An influencer will always prefer a platform which will provide them with plenty of chances to work with brands. This means that the more prominent platforms with more customers have an advantage. However, a smaller platform will have fewer customers but also less competition. Try to avoid fully automated sites which provide a list of thousands of influencers to the client to choose from.

- **Rate supervision:** Influencers, especially in the early phases of their career, find it extremely difficult to decide their service price. These platforms have clear guidance about the worth of an influencer for a transaction. At Obvious.ly, for instance, 90 per cent of the influencers receive free product rather than monetary compensation. Platforms such as Influenz specify a payment rate according to your Instagram following.

- **Tools:** Platforms provide influencers with tools to monitor their content on various platforms. Brands also use these tools to check the increase in engagement due to your posts.

- **FTC guidelines:** Knowledge about the FTC guidelines is still relatively weak among influencers. Platforms must make an effort to inform their influencers about such guidelines.

TapInfluence, for instance, has a post about FTC guidelines on its site, making it very clear to influencers (brands and agencies) that they need to abide by it.

- **Well-established community:** A useful platform must help the influencers level up their game and help them be part of a genuine community of influencers and brands.

Some other popular influencer platforms are AspireIQ, Upfluence, NeoReach and Chttrbox.

ASPIREIQ

AspireIQ's user-friendly interface which acts as an influencer discovery search engine makes it an excellent platform for brands and influencers alike. They currently have a database of 500,000 people, which they believe are authentic and experts in at least one niche.

Influencers need to apply to be a part of AspireIQ's influencer database. Profiles are critically examined before they are approved. The interface doesn't charge any fees or commission from the earnings and is available free. The platforms that it supports are Instagram, YouTube, Facebook, Twitter, Pinterest and blogs.

UPFLUENCE

It is a community of more than 3 million creators (influencers). Their proprietary algorithms index and update all the real-time profiles, with every content analysed for reach and engagement.

The Upfluence extension is free to install on Google Chrome. All you need to do is register your profile in its database. After adding the extension to Chrome, you can visit your profile and click on the Upfluence plug-in. It will allow you to use all the analytics tools.

The platforms it supports are Instagram, YouTube, Facebook, Twitch, TikTok, Twitter, Pinterest and blogs.

NEOREACH

Influencers don't even need to sign up for their service. NeoReach finds its influencers using a sophisticated algorithm that mines the social media and web for relevant data. Also, it has developed its method of calculating your ROI. They call it influencer media value (IMV), and it aims to show the real value of your influencer marketing campaigns. The platforms it supports are Facebook, Twitter, Instagram, YouTube, Pinterest and Snapchat.

CHTTRBOX

Chttrbox (pronounced Chatterbox) is a platform for brands to discover and collaborate with talented influencers (over 180,000) in India. You can set your fees as an influencer and decide which brand you want to work with. Also, it is free to join. The platform uses its algorithm to help you determine your social media value.

The platforms it supports are Instagram, YouTube, Twitter, Snapchat and Facebook.

In this chapter, we discussed some of the fundamental aspects of influencer marketing. In the upcoming chapters, we will explore more advanced strategies in influencer marketing.

CHAPTER 13

INFLUENCER TYPES: WHICH IS BEST?

In the last chapter, we discussed the basics of influencer marketing, why it is effective on social media, and how brands leverage them to promote their products. In this chapter, we will explore the types of influencers and the importance of collaborations between influencers.

TYPES OF INFLUENCERS

With close to half a million active Instagram influencers, it is essential to demarcate the influencers to promote a successful marketing campaign. Now, let's take a look at the types of influencers.

Celebrity

These are the 'big names' or celebrities in various industries. They are also called massive influencers, which suggests that their reach is enormous, and they are ideal for a brand awareness campaign. An example of an enormous influencer is Bollywood actor Ranveer Singh promoting Kotak Mahindra Bank's services through a video on his Instagram handle.

The actor announces that this is a paid collaboration at the top of the post itself. This is a great medium to ensure that your product is at the least put forth in front of 10–20 million people. Although a massive influencer is not too effective in sales conversions, they are suitable for reaching many people. In return, these influencers charge a tremendous amount to feature just a single post.

Macro Influencer

These influencers generally have followers between the range of 0.5 and 1 million on their social media platforms. We can call them a mini celebrity. Most brands leverage macro influencers, and some of the reasons for choosing them are as follows:

- They are cost-effective when compared to the massive influencers.
- They can drive more conversions and sales.
- They have loyal fan followers.

Micro Influencers

Generally, micro influencers have between 10,000 and 50,000 followers. It might seem that the audience is small, but it is counterbalanced by the loyal fan following that micro influencers have due to their expertise.

The best part is the engagement that these influencers get and their relatability with the audience. The point to note here is that the engagement rate in micro influencers is much higher than massive influencers. Influencers with 1,000 followers get a 6 per cent engagement rate compared to the engagement rate of 1.6 per cent for massive influencers.

Followers following ratio = Number of users who follow you/ Number of users you follow. This ratio is generally used on Instagram and Twitter to check how good your account is. For an average user, the ratio should be 0.7–2.5; but as we are looking for an influencer, a ratio of 2.5 would be miserable. Higher the ratio is, more is the power of the influencer. While macro influencers

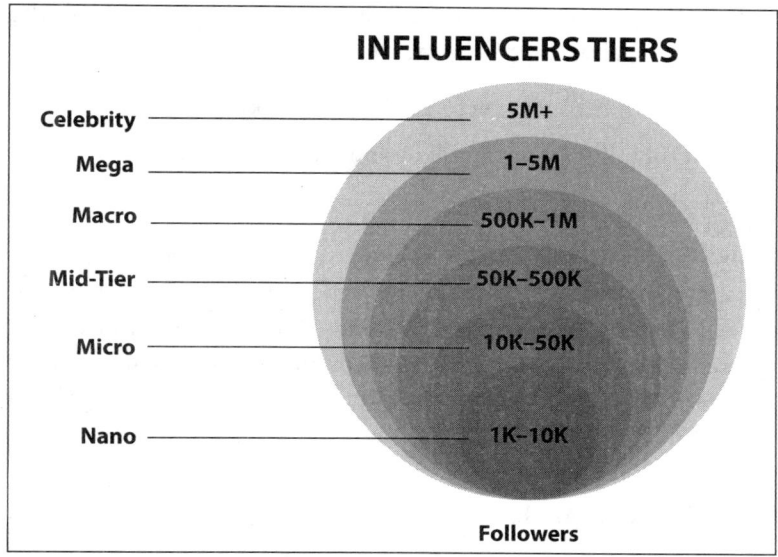

Figure 13.1: Types of Influencers
Source: https://senseimarketing.com/6-types-of-influencers/ (accessed on 3 January 2020).

should have a ratio of more than 10,000,[1] international celebrities have a ratio of more than 1 million.

Apart from the categories mentioned above, there are some subcategories, as shown in Figure 13.1.

Now, let's look at the most popular niches and the platforms on which the influencers promote these niches.

INFLUENCER MARKETING IN PROMINENT NICHES
Beauty

The cosmetics industry is projected to surpass $863 billion by 2024. Beauty influencers specialize in sharing how-to videos, tutorials

---

[1] https://brandequity.economictimes.indiatimes.com/news/marketing/how-influencer-marketing-is-battling-the-growing-menace-of-bots/71104985 accessed on 7 December 2021).

and product reviews. Since the industry revolves around visuals, the preferred social media platforms are as follows:

- Instagram (to show pictures of their work)
- YouTube (for how-to videos and tutorials)
- Facebook

Influencers can share a time-lapse of their lengthy work on Instagram or share it as an IGTV video (make sure it does not exceed 10–12 minutes). YouTube tends to be the central platform, where the exchange of valuable information between you and your audience occurs. So use other platforms to divert more people to your YouTube channel.

Health and Fitness

Globally, fitness has exploded into a nearly $100 billion industry in 2020, as more people are becoming obsessed with their health. Since this profession is about guidance and getting into good shape, the preferred social media platforms are as follows:

- Instagram (to post pictures of you and your workout and drive people to YouTube)
- YouTube (central platform to cover proper workouts and diets)
- Snapchat and TikTok (to show part of your workout to gain following) Facebook

Travel

Since the sector lures the audience with sparkling photographs and videos, the following are the preferred social media platforms:

- Instagram
- Snapchat and TikTok
- Blog

While some of the people focus more on pictures, others attract the audience with their creative writing.

Fashion

The worldwide fashion and apparel e-commerce industries were valued at almost $500 billion in 2020 (and predicted to grow to $713 billion by 2022). The following are the preferred platforms:

- Instagram
- Snapchat
- TikTok

Business

While this sector is a bit more formal and centres more on the quality of information than visuals, the following are the preferred mediums:

- Website (the centre of all information)
- LinkedIn (giving some information to attract an audience, and then leaving your website URL)
- Instagram (just for sharing via a picture the new content you posted on your website/LinkedIn)
- Facebook

Luxury/Lifestyle

The youth is attracted to luxurious products along with a lavish and vibrant lifestyle. This section mostly revolves around how the person leads a life of luxury. The exchange of valuable information is significantly less, and the audience is attracted to this sector because it is pleasing to the eyes. The following are the preferred social media platforms:

- Instagram
- Snapchat
- TikTok
- Facebook

The influencer must post animated pictures to make an impact.

Gaming

The gaming industry was worth $180 billion by 2021. With enhancements in technology such as augmented reality and artificial intelligence, the gaming experience is becoming fascinating. The competition in this segment is stiff. You need to have superior skills to be a gaming influencer. The following platforms are preferred:

- Twitch
- YouTube
- Facebook

The concept of livestreaming has accelerated the growth of gaming influencers.

Animals

The world loves animals. The pet care industry is forecasted to exceed $202 billion worldwide in the next few years. People are attracting huge audiences by sharing happy moments with their pets. The preferred social media platforms are as follows:

- Instagram
- Snapchat
- Facebook
- YouTube

If you don't mind making long videos of your pet, you can focus on YouTube. Else, the platform of Instagram is best for sharing vivid pictures. You can also write articles regarding how to take care of the pet, the best products for your pet, etc.

Family/Parenting

This industry involves posting content around your family or your baby. The innocence of babies (and their cuteness) attracts a massive audience to such content.

The following are the preferred platforms:

- Instagram
- Facebook
- Snapchat

Like the pet industry, you can also write blogs if you have enough content.

COLLABORATION BETWEEN INFLUENCERS

Sometimes, collaboration with other influencers can be a game changer for you. Brands do not mind investing money on multiple influencers simultaneously as the 'return on investment' (ROI) is high. The whole experience of getting to know other influencers and working with them can be quite insightful. Also, by collaborating, you get to access the other influencer's audience and make an entry into the community of experienced influencers. Since most of the brands opt for multiple influencers, the chances of getting recommended also increase.

FEAR OF SOCIAL MEDIA BOTS

A bot is a software application created to run automated tasks over the Internet. In social media, it is primarily used to automatically generate messages, follow other people, and create fake accounts to gain followers to a specific social media page. This activity is pretty standard on Instagram and Twitter, with some influencers and brands running greedy behind likes and followers. It is estimated that around 9–15 per cent of Twitter accounts may be bots.[2] Due to their high prowess in automation (including messaging), these bots are leveraged to propagate ideas and influence people towards a particular agenda—simply pseudo influencers! It is either spamming or blending in with groups, you have no idea that its software drives people like you towards action.

[2] http://www.Mediakix.com 6.https://www.distilnetworks.com/glossary/term/social-media-bots/ (accessed on 4 January 2020).

So how do these bots affect an influencer marketing campaign?

Mostly, in the case of influencer marketing, these bots take up the form of fake followers, which gives rise to 'influencer fraud'. What happens in influencer fraud is that despite having many followers, the brand gets unsatisfactory engagement and user activity. The main reason for this is bots. Many options are available online to 'buy' fake followers such as Buzzoid and Stormlikes.net. A hack that influencers with fake followers deploy uses generic 'hashtags', especially in the case of Instagram. The bot software is designed to identify these hashtags and bring about automated interaction in likes. A recent report from the Institute of Contemporary Music Performance (ICMP) revealed that several celebrities, and significant influencers, have many fake followers on platforms such as Instagram.

Interestingly, these celebrities are some of the most expensive ones too, as they charge based on the number of followers. That is why brands are now moving away from relying too much on the number of followers of an influencer while signing them up.

There are multiple ways to identify bots.

- Although this can be leveraged only for influencers with a fair amount of fan following (not very much suitable for micro influencers), it still acts as a check for the influencer's credibility. If you look at some profiles on Instagram and Twitter, you'll find a blue certification badge which announces that the influencer's account is verified, and the account user is not a bot. But not much information about the followers is gathered. As an influencer, try to get a blue tick by getting your ID verified.

- People try to figure out an account's authenticity by comparing the number of likes/comments on that account's post and its number of followers. If an account has followers in millions and likes in a hundred, then it looks suspicious. Do note that this trick gives an idea about the use of bots. The use of the software is recommended to get a clear picture.

- Tracking the follower growth by using tools like Social Blade can be advantageous. They let us know all the details of any social media account. You just need to plug in the URL in the space given, and you are ready to analyse the account.

- Experts feel that a legitimate influencer account is the one that has a stable and gradual growth over time. In a situation where an influencer suddenly gains 15,000 followers overnight, you can conclude that the influencers have 'paid' for the followers.
- You can spot bots through the comments section. Check for generic comments such as 'Great' and 'Nice pic'. These comments are mostly associated with bots rather than actual humans.

Lastly, we will consider collaboration with multiple influencers. In general, you can rest assured that the influencer is indeed genuine if you find collaborative content. As no one wants to spoil their reputation by collaborating with a fake influencer, brands can be sure that the influencers are real.

CHAPTER 14

HOW TO BECOME AN INFLUENCER?

In the last chapter, we looked at different influencers' types and the whole process of selecting an influencer from the brand's point of view. Now, it's time to get familiar with the process of being an influencer in detail.

As an influencer, it is always crucial to keep this quote in mind. In the words of Seth Godin, an American author, 'People do not buy goods and services; they buy relations, stories, and magic.' Your treasure as an influencer is your relationship with your audience. Never do anything to jeopardize it! So holding on to this thought, let's start the journey of becoming a renowned influencer.

Two approaches can be followed while deciding the platforms you are going to join.

- Be everywhere
- Choose one

BE EVERYWHERE
Pros of the 'Be Everywhere' Approach

- You will reach audiences that prefer one platform over another. If you are on Twitter, YouTube, and Instagram, you can communicate with people who love short and witty texts, people who love in-detail videos and people who are fond of great pictures, all at the same time.

- People who follow you on multiple networks will come across your message numerous times, without even trying.
- Being on more platforms makes you look more experienced and professional.

The biggest con is the time it takes to maintain your presence on different platforms in the long run. Making good-quality content for every platform is challenging for a person to achieve in the long term. This method works if you have a small content team which can work on content for different platforms in a parallel manner.

CHOOSE ONE
Pros of the 'Choose One' Approach

- You need to focus on only one kind of content—videos for YouTube, clippings for TikTok and pictures for Instagram/Pinterest. It makes it easier to stay consistent and learn much more about your customer's needs around that platform.
- It is easier to build a social presence on one platform, making it easier to gain followers on other platforms. This also acts as your social proof. It is better to have 2,000 followers on one platform than to have 400 followers each on 5 platforms.
- Since you only have one platform to manage, you can respond faster to your audience's questions.

The con of this is that you can only focus on the audience present on that platform. It is also risky as you are putting all your eggs in one basket, and you are at the mercy of that platform's policies. But this approach is favoured by people who maintain their channel and social presence entirely on their own.

NICHE

The first thing to figure out is your niche. All your content will revolve around it. If you want people to pay attention to your content, then you need to go in-depth to capture the little details.

Some of the popular niche categories are fashion, health, sports, travel, entertainment, tech and business, which we discussed in the previous chapter.

Importance of Passion

The key to beat the immense competition which comes with being an influencer is passion. Be passionate about every part of your journey, especially your niche. Passion will encourage you to leave no stone unturned. For example, if you are excited about new smartphones, then mobile technology can be your niche.

Importance of Personal Touch

You need to put your personality in your content. This is essential. Let's understand this with an example. You need to know about your niche more than the average audience, which is a fundamental requirement. Now, humans tend to favour those people who value the same things you value. For example, people who love Apple products will approve of people who prefer Apple products. This is because they feel understood and appreciated.

This goes for almost everything. Assuming you provide adequate information regularly, your real audience will continue to follow you because of the way you present your content and your personal preferences.

So adding your personality and improvising your content accordingly are necessary to thrive.

Suppose you are a student in the niche of smartphones, then while reviewing phones, you can focus on things which matter the most to students and how some features can help students.

Choosing the Right Platform

Now that you have figured out your niche, it's time to choose the platform to connect with your target audience. The right platform ensures that your audience finds your content.

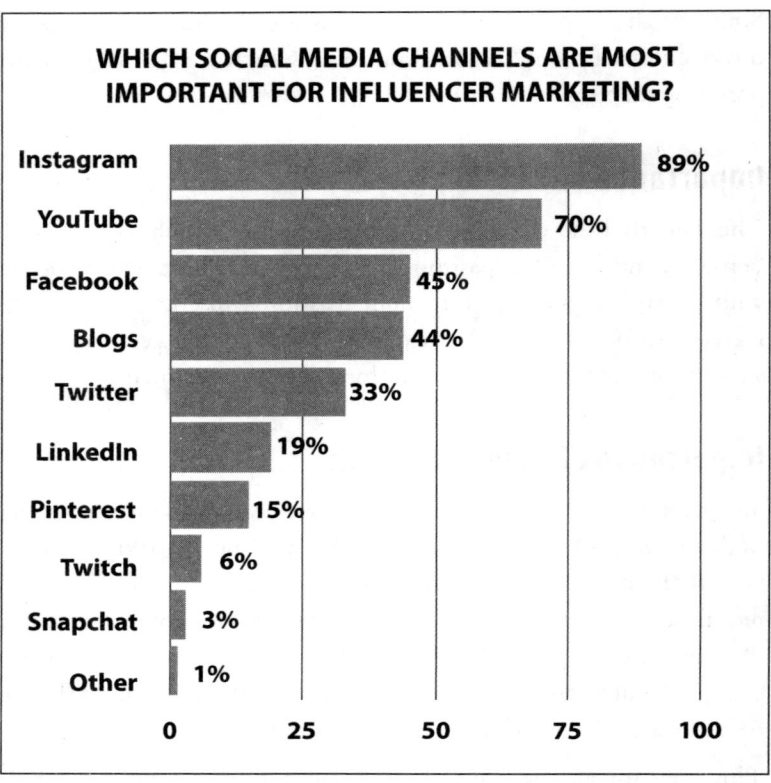

Figure 14.1: Social Media Platforms Preferred by Influencers

Source: https://mediakix.com/blog/category/influencer-marketing (accessed on 7 July 2020).

Figure 14.1 shows that 89 per cent of the influencers prefer Instagram over other platforms to share their content. Instagram's huge dominance is due to its sparkling interface which nudges people to post highly visual content along with a catchy caption. Options such as stories and IGTV make Instagram an excellent platform for video content too.

However, choose the platform that your audience uses. To figure out the right platform, you need to recognize your target audience. Try to figure out the traits that define your audience. For example, if you want to connect with a young audience interested in gaming, you should prefer Twitch and YouTube over Instagram. Similarly, if you target youth with a knack for videos, platforms such as Snapchat, Instagram and TikTok are the appropriate choices.

So ask yourself the following questions to get a better understanding of your target audience. What is their age, and which platforms do they use?

Which channel is your competition using to promote their content?

What type of content do you intend to create in the long term? What is the type of content that you can comfortably create?

Now, let's look at some popular platforms and how they differ from each other

TIKTOK

This platform revolves around the short clip format, mainly 15 seconds video. Also, you don't need a professional camera to make videos on it. Since the video's length is short, niches such as business-to-business marketing and finance aren't fit for it. Also, the format of content shared on it is mostly informal. Famous influencers belong to dance, beauty (time-lapse videos and final look shot), humour and cooking.

The most significant factor in the success of TikTok is the level of engagement from the audience. The exciting challenges and the ease of putting a video on TikTok urge millions of users to take part in it. This could not be achieved on YouTube, mainly because of the effort it takes to make a decent video for YouTube.

INSTAGRAM

Instagram is the king of social media platforms. It has over 1 billion active users worldwide. The platform is suitable for almost every type of content. While it revolves around pictures and short videos, the evolution of stories and IGTV videos makes it quite useful for practically every industry. As of April 2020, Instagram is one of the most popular social networks worldwide, especially among young adults.[1]

With almost 500,000 daily users and around 25 million business profiles, it is the best platform for businesses. The primary reason for its success is that it is the most agile platform of all. From stories to posts and IGTV videos, it provides numerous ways of producing a new form of content.

YouTube

When it comes to a good video-sharing platform, YouTube wins fair and square. It has more than 2 billion logged-in monthly users.[2]

It is popular in beauty, gaming, humour, tech, health and fitness, and cooking. Since it is the earliest of all platforms, it caters to a massive audience. Although hashtag challenges and user-generated content (UGC) cannot be done, the YouTube partner programme makes up for it. It is the only platform that pays for attracting an audience.

TWITTER

Twitter has 330 million monthly active users and 145 million daily users worldwide. A total of 1.3 billion accounts have been created.[3]

Unlike other platforms focusing on visuals, Twitter focuses on a short form of text. It allows you to write only 280 characters and enables you to post pictures and videos. What makes Twitter different is everyone is on it, from politicians to people in business to actors, everyone shares their opinion on Twitter.

Celebrity niche, world news niche and health niche are among the most popular niches on it.

---

[1] https://www.statista.com/statistics/578364/countrieswithmostInstagramusers/#:~:text=Instagram's%20popularity,active%20users%20in%20June%202018 (accessed on 7 July 2020).

[2] https://blog.hootsuite.com/youtube-stats-marketers/#user (accessed on 7 July 2020).

[3] https://www.brandwatch.com/blog/twitterstatsandstatistics/#:~:text=Twitter%20user (accessed on 7 December 2021).

FACEBOOK

With Facebook, users can not only post comments and photos, but they can also look through their local news feeds, create live videos, make an event plan, send messages to friends, ask for recommendations, and buy or sell items. This is by far the broadest social media platform. Facebook has over 2.6 billion monthly active users.5

Some of the popular niches are fitness and weight loss, health, dating and relationships, pets, self-improvement, wealth building through investing, making money on the Internet and beauty treatments.

For example, if your niche is fashion, then most of your content will be pictures and videos. So Instagram and Snapchat are apt platforms for you. It is advised to have your presence on two–three social media platforms. One is your primary platform, and the other platforms' existence is to direct people to your primary social media account.

CONTENT STRATEGY

Once you figure out the platform, you are just a step away from reaching your target audience. The first thing to do is have a catchy name for your channel. Some of the famous examples would be Unbox Therapy, TechnicalGuruji and GeekyRanjit. Make it appealing enough that it sticks with people.

Now, you need to focus on your content thoroughly. High-quality, unique content is imperative to succeed as an influencer. This guarantees that your audience will have a pleasant experience interacting with your content.

To post high-quality content regularly for a long time, it is necessary to have a strategy. Also, you need to leverage all types of options that the platform offers, such as stories, photos and videos.

Some influencers follow the rule of thirds. It requires you to split your social media posts into three parts:

- One-third of your posts are your content.
- One-third of your posts are for sharing content from others.

- One-third of your posts are personal interactions which build your brand.

The best way to capture someone's attention is to create content on stuff they care about. You need to focus your content on the problems faced by your audience. To find your target audience's pain points effectively, here are a few tricks that will help you.

- Websites like AnswerThePublic provide you with all the trending questions around the keyword entered.
- The comment section of your videos/posts is where your audience will interact with you directly. You will find many new ideas for your content.
- Quora and Reddit are great places to hunt for new ideas for your content. Keep your search around keywords strongly connected with your niche.
- Follow your competition, especially the experienced players in your niche. Notice the content that they are focusing on.

Also, to continually post new stuff in your niche, you need to keep up with your niche's latest information. Reading research papers, blog posts, watching YouTube videos, etc., can take up a lot of your time. Tools like Feedly and Nuzzel can be quite helpful.

Feedly lets you access it for free, and its paid service starts at as low as $6 per month. The use of such tools makes the task of keeping up with new information comfortable.

As mentioned earlier, your asset as an influencer is your connection with your audience. So to develop a bond, nudge your viewers to drop a comment about the content shown or any problem they are facing. When they do comment, respectfully respond to them. Thank them for taking out some time to leave feedback on your work.

According to TechCrunch, Instagram engages more than 700 million users each month. Other stats tell us that 63 per cent of users log in at least once a day. It witnesses a total of 95 million photos and videos every single day. So the algorithm of Instagram and every other social media platform is designed to filter out and present high-quality content to its users.

So whenever you post something on any social media platform, rather than showing your post to all your followers, the post goes through a micro test. It is shown to a smaller audience (some of your followers), and if the ratio of the number of likes to the number of views is healthy, it presents the post to a broader audience. If a video is well received by a smaller audience, it is expected to deliver the same result when shown to a bigger audience.

When given an option to choose between two videos, one has 5k likes, and the other has 200 likes. Most of the people go with the one with maximum likes. If users like your content, they will check your profile.

Around 200 million Instagram users visit at least one business profile daily. You need to post the content according to your profile and choosing the right hashtags so that users visit your profile and then follow you.

Know Your Digital Marketing Tools

You're not on your Instagram marketing journey alone and without help. Some digital marketing tools that our team found useful are as follows.

1. **Top Tags:** Top Tags has a user-friendly interface with the ability to mix hashtags of different categories to get the most relevant hashtags.

2. **HashMe hashtag generator:** This tool lets you simply upload the picture and instantly get the best hashtags on Instagram tailored for your post. This allows the influencers to broaden their spectrum around the hashtags they can leverage.

3. **Hashtastic:** Hashtastic is a website which takes your post's topic and the average number of likes that you get per post as inputs to give you the most suitable hashtags. The app provides a more personalized approach to delivering the right hashtags by considering your current social media position.

Know How to Enhance Your Post

While it is crucial to include hashtags to increase your post's chances of getting popular, it is equally important to make sure you have an engaging post in the first place. Here are some tips to augment your post's quality so that hashtags will further enhance its propagation.

1. **Make it bright:** Humans are programmed to notice things brighter than the background, which is why Instagram's wall is all grey. Use the filters to make the picture more vivid and contrasted (in a limited way, as we don't want to mislead people!).

2. **A picture speaks a thousand words:** Avoid using too many words, and try your best to convey as much meaning as possible with images.

3. **Less is more:** Write only what is necessary and make sure you don't repeat anything. Your caption should complement your image.

Know the Ladder

Conquer the lower rungs of the ladder before moving on to the next one.

Imagine the different hashtags in successive order of how many posts each hashtag contains, like the rungs of a ladder. Let's take an example involving hashtags for painting.

You have to conquer the hashtag with 144k posts first before moving on to stand out in the hashtags with 507k or 89M posts.

If you do well in 144k posts, you are likely to do well later in 507k and further in 89M posts, consequently exposing your channel to a larger and more varied audience.

#Dontusetoolonghashtags

It will be as difficult to read long hashtags as it was for you to read this heading. Other people will only use your hashtags if it is short, catchy and straightforward.

Hashtags which are too long are more prone to misunderstanding, putting the brand in really embarrassing positions.

It is an art to use hashtags and also not seem too aggressive. One way is to put a few dots in the next five to six lines of a caption and then put the hashtags. This puts the 'read more' option, and the viewer only sees the caption. Another way is to put the hashtags in the comments section. Note that Instagram only allows a total of 30 hashtags on a post. This includes the hashtags in the comments as well.

Avoid using hashtags like #Follow4follow and #likes4likes. These hashtags look insensitive and show desperation. The following are some unhealthy practices you should avoid.

1. Avoid using banned hashtags. If you feel that the hashtag is banned, search it on Instagram. If it doesn't show any result, it means it is banned either temporarily or permanently. For example, Instagram banned Kansas because too many users were using it on posts that violated Instagram's community guidelines.

2. Don't use software that violates Instagram's terms of service. If you use software that automatically posts to Instagram for you, make sure it isn't violating Instagram's terms of service. You could be at risk of getting your entire Instagram account banned. Instagram uses technology to detect bot activity which automatically likes, comments and posts, so stay away from bots.

3. Avoid significant rise in account activity. Instagram has a limit of how many posts you can like and comment, and people you can follow/unfollow in a period. This is introduced to detect bot behaviour with excessive likes or follows. If you follow 100 accounts suddenly, Instagram might interpret this as 'bot activity' and ban your account as a result.

4. Avoid getting reported by other users. It immediately puts you on Instagram's radar for suspicious activity.

5. Try using some new hashtags every time, even if you feel the previous ones were successful.

Using Hashtags in Your Bio

The use of hashtags isn't limited to posts. You can also use hashtags in your bio. You can use hashtags in your bio to give your audience a broad idea about your profile. The people who see your bio will get a better idea about your niche if you include hashtags in your bio.

Also, when you use hashtags in your bio, there are more chances to get an audience for your post.

By adding hashtags in your bio, you are making your profile easy to discover.

User-generated Content

If you are already an influencer (or an affiliate marketer) or you want to be one, then you need to exploit this wild card. UGC is more attractive and effective than other forms of media. It is the perfect way of having two-way communication with your audience. It can be achieved via hashtags, challenges and contests. Brands are desperate for such influencers these days.

Apart from UGC, most customers want the brands to demonstrate that they understand and care about them before they are going to consider purchasing. This can be inferred from the basic need of human beings to seek approval and be understood.[4] This applies to freelancers as well. Freelancers must have a deep sense of connection and care for their clients and prospects.

REGULATIONS IN INFLUENCER MARKETING

The Advertising Standards Council of India (ASCI) is framing disclosure rules for social media influencers who promote products

---

[4] http://www.sproutsocial.com (accessed on 7 July 2020).

on the Internet.[5] The influencer market is estimated at $75–150 million per year in India and is proliferating.

The wake-up call was when the Fyre Festival in 2017 failed. All the famous influencers promoted the festival as if they were genuinely excited about it (they were given festival tickets in payment). It would not have been an issue if the festival was anything like it was promised. It was a total disaster, which raised questions on how the entire influencer marketing worked.

FTC Guidelines[6]

In 2017, FTC decided to be more proactive and sent letters to 90 influencers to clearly and conspicuously disclose any relationships they had with brands when they endorsed social media products. These letters resulted from complaints to FTC by various organizations concerned about the lack of transparency and honesty in some social media posts. It acted as a wake-up call for the influencer industry. There was an explicit mention of Instagram in the letter, and it also mentioned how the mobile users could only see the first three lines of the post (and had to click on 'Read more' to read the entire caption). Since most users focus on the pictures and ignore the latter part of the caption while using the application, they miss out on disclosing any sponsorship by the influencer later in the caption. This led to Instagram introducing the 'Paid Partnership' feature to make it easier to disclose paid arrangements (if any).

FTC defines endorsement as to any statement, demonstration, or depiction of name or signature identifying an individual or a company that consumers are likely to believe reflects the opinion of a party other than the sponsoring advertiser.

It is important to remember that to be considered an endorser here, the influencer must benefit. An influencer doesn't qualify

---

[5] https://www.businesstoday.in/current/corporate/social-media-influencer-to-be-soon-on-advertising-regulators-radar-asci-advertising-standards-council-of-india/story/383739.html (accessed on 7 July 2020).

[6] https://www.ftc.gov/system/files/documents/plain-language/1001a-influencer-guide-508_1.pdf (accessed on 21 February 2022).

as an endorser if they present comments on the product without receiving anything in return.

FTC defines an expert as being 'an individual, group, or institution possessing, as a result of experience, study, or training, knowledge of a particular subject, which knowledge is superior to what ordinary individuals generally acquire'.

Most of the influencers, if not all, qualify as an expert according to this definition. FTC used various examples to explain the regulations better. They talked about a consumer who buys a new brand of dog food and writes about how it has improved their dog's health. They gave three possible scenarios:

1. The blogger pays for the food, likes it and praises it in their blog—not an endorsement

2. The blogger gets the food for free because they used a loyalty coupon from their local supermarket—not an endorsement

3. The blogger receives free dog food through network marketing and writes a positive review of it—an endorsement.

Also, the guidelines mentioned that the advertisement must reflect the honest opinion of the endorser. An online influencer has to be extra careful that they don't mislead their audiences with dishonest statements.

The guidelines gave an example of a campaign for skincare products using influential beauty bloggers. The advertiser requested the bloggers to try out a new body lotion and write a review of the product. Suppose that a blogger alone claims in their review that the cream cures eczema and recommends it to people who suffer from the condition.

In this situation, both the blogger and the advertiser (even though the advertiser never made this claim) are accountable for making false representations about the lotion. FTC mentioned that the brand must monitor posts and stop the influencers from making false claims as soon as they get to know about it.

Consumer Endorsement

FTC also provided guidelines for consumer endorsement. If a consumer is paid to share their experience of using a product, and they are depicted as a typical user, other users should also get matching results. These endorsement rules apply only when there is an exchange of money or product.

It is acceptable for a user to share views different from other users, provided the company does not pay the user. For example, an influencer reviewing a new smartphone from Samsung is allowed to say that they disliked the product, provided no one pays them to say so.

Also, the guidelines mandate clear scientific evidence to back the claims of product performance, and only the customer's testimony is not sufficient. For example, if a company claims that the product increases height, it must provide proper scientific proof to support it.

Another area is to provide comprehensive information when endorsing any claims about the product. For example, it will not be enough for an endorser of weight loss shakes to claim that they lost 110 pounds in six months by consuming the shake (even if they had) unless they also mentions all the other factors such as diet change and increased exercise which could also contribute to the weight loss.

Expert Signature

If an influencer is represented as an expert on a subject, it means that they should have relevant experience and qualifications.

Disclosure of Material Connections

If you receive money to write a post, status, tweet or share an image, a video or virtually anything else online where you are promoting a good or service, you must make it very clear to your audience.

'When there exists a connection between the endorser and the seller of the advertised product that might materially affect the weight or credibility of the endorsement, such connection must be fully disclosed,' states FTC.

It doesn't matter how you disclose it, but it must be clear and unambiguous. You can't hide it behind a 'More' link, or you can't assume that people know what a #sp hashtag means. Instagram's 'Paid Partnership' subheader is a good move in the right direction. It clearly discloses that the content is the result of monetary deal between the brand and the influencer.

ANALYSE

The journey to be a successful influencer is to keep optimizing your strategies. The first step to optimization is to analyse how your content has performed. Most of the apps come with in-built insights to help influencers.

Now that you are familiar with everything, there is to know about influencer marketing; there is still something that you ought to know. That is the value of patience and consistency. There is no shortcut to success. You need to keep working towards your goal. Believe that things will work out even if situations force you to think they won't.

- You can also mix two or more niches. Just make sure that it makes sense. For example, you can combine travel with fashion or lifestyle.
- Host different types of contests and giveaways to always keep your audience on toes.
- Happy emotions (joy, awe, laughter and amusement) drive 71 per cent of the campaigns. So make sure that your content is more on the happy side (refer to Figure 14.2 for emotions that make content go viral).

Now that we know enough about all the three professions, let us see how they are similar.

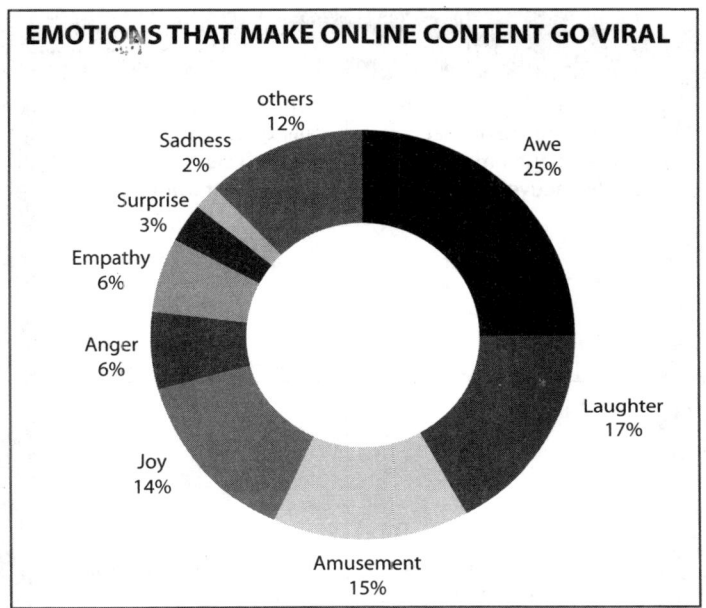

Figure 14.2: Emotions That Make Content Go Viral

Source: https://www.ftc.gov/system/files/documents/plain-language/1001a-influencer-guide- 5081.pdf (accessed on 7 July 2020).

Freelancing and Affiliate Marketing

While freelancing can be done in many fields, content writing and web development are the most prominent sectors. They will also open up the opportunity for you in affiliate marketing. Advanced affiliate marketers do look for freelancers to write content for one of their many websites. The same goes for web development. As your skills sharpen, you can get your domain and start your affiliate journey. There is no denying that freelancing is an excellent profession in itself, but it is always good to have multiple sources of income.

Affiliate Marketing and Influencer Marketing

These two are so incredibly similar that sometimes it isn't possible to distinguish between them. For example, when you give your

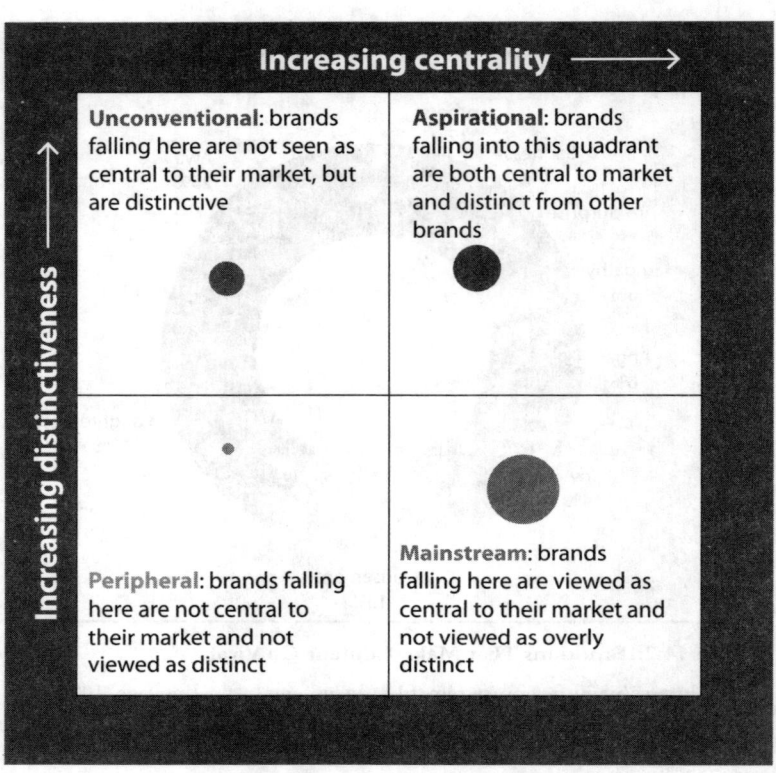

Figure 14.3: Framework for Analysing Brands
Source: https://www.b2binternationalusa.com/2018/08/15/c-d-mapping-a-different-approach- to-brand-mapping/ (accessed on 7 July 2020).

audience an honest review for a new smartphone on a blog, you can provide affiliate links for that phone. This is affiliate marketing. When a brand approaches you to improve its awareness and produce content about it, it is influencer marketing. Almost all the influencers are affiliate marketers.

We can apply a framework to analyse brands (refer to Figure 14.3). It can also be applied to human brands to understand the importance of personality and unique content for influencers, affiliate marketers and freelancers. It shows that human brands can be analysed based on two dimensions: centrality and distinctiveness. Centrality indicates how strong the positioning in the niche is. Distinctiveness means how unique or different the influencer is. Continually writing about things happening around your niche can increase centrality, but a few can create distinct content. An excellent example of such an influencer is TechnicalGuruji. He is a tech enthusiast who is loved for his extreme interest in new technology and the super catchy phrases he uses in every video, making him distinct. Freelancing content writers often add such catchy slangs to make their content look unique and relatable to the audience. As an influencer, identify your personality—who are you as a person: quirky, sincere, genuine, professional, friendly, irreverent, serious, humorous, warm, male/female, and young/old. Once you have identified, stay true to your personality by using consistent tonality in your content.

CHAPTER 15

HOW E-COMMERCE MAKES MONEY

Many people make a lot of money and live extraordinary lives from their online stores. If you are looking forward to making some extra cash and fill your wallet with the power of the Internet, this content is for you.

You need to start with an online store or website and understand some online marketing tactics to drive revenues. Once you are able to do this, you will reap great benefits. E-commerce websites are perhaps one of the primary sources of making money online. If you have some content- and product-rich website, there is a way to make money online.

You need to have an e-commerce platform to develop a virtual experience which enables you to trade and make sales—the place where your potential clients are or where they prefer to shop.

While it is common to think that an e-commerce platform is merely a medium for listing products and accepting payments online, a trustworthy e-commerce platform has to be much more than that.

An e-commerce platform is expected to be an all-in-one business control centre which permits you to keep a hold on everything from inventory to marketing. It must permit you to accept payments and also provide you a flawless access to any tool that you may require for selling online.

Since the success of any Internet business depends heavily on your website visitors, it is imperative that you learn the art of driving website traffic through various online marketing channels such as Google's organic search, social media and paid ads. Remember that half of your work is done once you have an idea of the multiple tips for increasing web traffic.

WHAT DIFFERENT TYPES OF E-COMMERCE PLATFORMS EXIST?

In order to make your online store available to the masses, you must own a hosting solution. Your personal information is stored on a server through hosting, which in turn permits virtual customers to explore your site and content.

Each and every website in the world needs to be hosted somewhere, which implies that it boasts of a dedicated server space from a specific provider. Several e-commerce platforms have built-in hosting, while others require you to utilize open-source hosting or self-hosting.

Hosting

Some website creators provide you with a platform for hosting. In such scenarios, you don't need to be stressed about any self or third-party hosting and the extra charges involved.

For example, Shopify stores have website hosting in all their plans. As a result, all its updates are absolutely flawless and automatic and you will always have a site which is up to date. Plus, you will have more free time to concentrate on managing your online business rather than putting out fires triggered by downtime and fixing bugs.

Self-hosting

Self-hosted, better known as the non-hosted, e-commerce platforms refer to the ones which require merchants to utilize their own server space or rent the space from any leading hosting provider, making the day-to-day site management difficult since you are in charge of maintenance, updates, bug fixes and the internal resources which can be placed elsewhere.

These are usually open-sourced, and you need to utilize third-party services to store your website data. Now, since the third-party sources charge a fee for their services, these expenses add up quickly. These services usually employ a tiered pricing structure. As a result, the ones with the lowest plans don't receive a lot of customer support. This can get you caught up in really important moments, like a surge in traffic following an unexpected press coverage.

DO WE NEED A PERFECT E-COMMERCE PLATFORM?

After all, there's no finest option for all, so identify the ideal e-commerce platform which gives your potential customers a good e-commerce experience so that they can shop with ease.

Consider all the various business tools those platforms have to offer, beyond simply a fantastic virtual store builder. It is usually valuable to utilize a flawlessly integrated ecosystem comprising of your store, point of sale (POS), transaction processor and even small business lender.

The perfect e-commerce platform depends on your own unique business model idea and the desired growth plan. Here's a detailed summary of a few of the finest e-commerce platforms which will help you choose the best option for your business.

Wix

Wix is an easy, customer-friendly, drag-and-drop website-builder application or tool which offers many features such as domain name registration, customizable templates and web hosting; you can effortlessly and quickly build an essential free website, but you will need to use a premium plan to play around with Wix's e-commerce features.

As far as e-commerce functionality is concerned, Wix has some effective tools. For example, it permits traders to track their orders, accept online payments, create abandoned cart campaigns and sell on multiple channels.

However, it does lack a few essential features which are otherwise needed for product-based businesses in particular. Shortcomings are the non-existence of low stock alerts and some crucial inventory management features. You will require a platform with more efficient inventory-tracking tools if you have more than 10 products. And you need to employ a third-party app for social commerce integrations.

Shopify

Shopify possesses an entire set of features which assist one in managing and tackling each and every domain of your business and an application store with more than 4,000 apps which help you in customizing the virtual experience for your customers and team members.

BigCommerce

BigCommerce is an e-commerce platform which is apt for corporation-level software companies. Just like Shopify and Wix, BigCommerce offers web hosting and lots of options for customization. But one cannot register their domain name through BigCommerce, so they need to register somewhere else and then port it over.

Important features include advanced SEO tools, selling, and multichannel sales on social and third-party marketplaces. But with these international features also comes the challenge of complexity.

Now, it is about identifying the finest and the most accessible platform for commerce—from online to in-store and everything in between.

This conveys that you need a premier virtual store and a suite of business management tools. You must find an easy-to-use medium which continuously updates its technology and remains at the forefront of the curve. A website builder is definitely so much more than just a platform where you can do business—it can also be a means for higher growth.

While analysing the given choices, consider the following storylines:

- I have to sell my products offline and online, to all my clients—irrespective of where they are—and accept payments for the same.
- I have to supply my services to my clients in the best way possible.
- I have to engage my present and potential clients to bloom my business.
- I have to handle my business on day-to-day basis, managing everything from taking care of my finances to checking if my strategies are working, learning new plans and getting technical support whenever needed.

WHICH IS THE BEST?

Shopify is no doubt the finest platform available for e-commerce. One can also trade directly through their website, at their own retail store, on social media and third-party marketplaces as a result of their advanced platform which comes with complementary tools and features for multichannel selling.

Also, Shopify manages all your business features—you can rely on their premier suite of business tools to build an all-in-one business command centre.

Shop Pay easily manages payment procedures, Shopify Point of Sale administers sales in-person and Shopify Fulfillment helps in getting the products into clients' hands.

And those are just a few of the big list of efficient apps and tools which work together seamlessly as part of the Shopify ecosystem. In addition, you can tap into the extensive list of third-party apps which can extend your experience with Shopify even further.

Using these effective features, you can also set up your own online business even with little technical knowledge and also expand to an international online brand without changing platforms along the way.

CHOOSING THE RIGHT PRODUCT TO SELL

Online markets are still booming with ample opportunities. Still, there are billions and billions of dollars to be made in e-commerce, so there is no surprise that brand new companies are popping up every day.

One of the biggest obstacles newbie entrepreneurs face is recognizing economical, on-demand products which will sell, be it a single one or an entire line of products which can fill a niche market.

Developing product ideas is undoubtedly tricky, and the significance of selling a product which customers want can trap the most motivated ones in analysis paralysis. Moreover, it usually feels like anything and everything you could possibly sell is already there in the market—not to mention that in reality there will always be huge competition in the most popular niches.

But there are a lot of golden examples to prove that new products are constantly being launched successfully. Hence, I have jotted down a short list of practical ways to identify products to sell in your store to get you started.

Let us discuss each of these strategies in more detail.

Solving a Consumer Problem

Solving a consumer problem is always an efficient way to create a product which people will buy. Solving customer pain points is usually about addressing frustrating experiences with the existing products.

It is worth paying careful attention if you come across similar frustrations with an available line of products. Awareness of the pain points and minor annoyances in day-to-day life could be exactly what you require to start thinking about your next billion-dollar product idea.

Go with Your Personal Passion

While deciding a niche on the basis of your own interests has inherent risks, it certainly isn't a pathway to disaster. On the contrary, utilizing your knowledge to develop a unique product might be highly profitable.

Take Your Professional Work Experience into Account

Has working in a specific field assisted you in learning the nuances? Perhaps you have a specific skill or experience which gives you an edge over others in a particular subject. Doing business online is an incredible way to enter the market with an advantage which is not easy for others to copy.

Leveraging Trends in the Early Stages

Identifying a trend early can bring in a lot of advantages for a new business. It enables you to make a name for yourself in the marketplace and validate yourself as a leader even before others have the chance. And due to the nature of digital marketing, your paid expenses are likely to be lower, and the opportunities to increase long-term SEO traffic will be plentiful.

Finding Products with a Higher Profit Margin

Products with the most negligible overhead are low-risk entry points because higher profit margins are easier to achieve than more expensive products. However, when pricing your products, you need to consider all the resources you have put in to sell your product, which is also your cost of goods sold (COGS).

In addition to the cost of building the product, you need to consider the price to promote, maintenance cost and even shipping cost. Therefore, identify inexpensive items which will give a high ROI. Remember that lightweight items are low-priced to ship, and just because any product is affordable to buy in bulk doesn't necessarily imply that you can get it for the highest ROI.

Deciding the ideal product or the best product category might be critical to your success. The products you select will shape your whole business, starting from marketing to shipping to pricing and product development.

One final reminder: Don't hesitate to consider smaller product categories and niches. Although a niche is actually a smaller subset of a wider variety with fewer customers overall, it usually makes up for this shortcoming.

GETTING TO KNOW YOUR POTENTIAL AUDIENCE

Introducing any new brand, product or service carries a great deal of risk. You can minimize this risk and drive your brand marketing efforts in the most effective way by understanding the whole market landscape. Identifying the right audience for your brand is like the first step, simple yet significant. Initially, broad strategies tend to be less impactful than highly specialized ones.

Thus, before starting your brand marketing, define your target audience, the particular groups you can expect to buy your product or service. Next, you will understand your current and potential clients.

SEGMENTING YOUR TARGET MARKET

Now that you have effectively identified your potential market, it is time to enhance your strategy. And this is where the target market segmentation comes into play. Market segmentation aims to provide more personalized marketing content to a particular group in your potential market. Common types of targeting are as follows.

Demographic: This implies that you segment your target audience on the basis of demographic information, which includes age, gender, income level, relationship status, etc. Study your customer details and observe if you notice any patterns. For instance, your consumers may be primarily women with disposable income.

Psychographic: Segment your audience on the basis of psychological factors such as social status, lifestyle, opinions, interests and activities. For instance, knowing that your customers are huge sports fans, you can devise your advertising around the game day.

Geographic: This concentrates on targeting on the basis of where they live. Common geographic segments can be state, region, local and country. For example, if most of your audience lives in Tamil Nadu, then marketing winter items may not be appropriate for that audience.

Behaviour: This kind of targeting classifies audiences on the basis of user's interactions with your brand. For instance, if you have an e-commerce business, you can create a list of users who have not made any purchase in last 60 days and retarget them with an email campaign in order to try and win them back.

The segmentation of target market enables efficient marketing with impactful spending and better user loyalty. With segmentation, you send relevant information only to target groups who are particularly interested in it. Your subscribers will get tired of receiving any material which is futile for them if you send all your content to your entire contact list.

CONDUCTING MARKET RESEARCH

Through primary and secondary market research, you may get information about your targeted audience. Primary research refers to learning about customer buying habits through direct contacts, which is discussed further.

Surveys

Distributing surveys to prospects on paper, email or web-based services might help you collect valuable data directly from your customers. For example, you can enquire them about previous products and strategies they liked and later utilize the feedback for your upcoming marketing campaign.

Interviews

Talk to trustworthy people whose buying habits are ideal for your business. Since it is more traditional and straightforward compared to a survey, it gives you honest answers for your marketing campaigns.

Focus Groups

Get small group feedback tailored to your client profile through interactive meetings and discussions.

Don't overlook existing customers as a source of information. When applied to customers, the same three methods help you analyse your target audience and lead you to enhanced service skills.

Do you ever ask shoppers to fill out forms or drop comments when they buy your product or service? They might be happy to answer questions about their age, location and shopping preferences. Invite them to volunteer to share information.

Evaluate Your Offers

After creating a complete customer profile, the very next step is to imagine your products or services from a new perspective. Question yourself what you know about your target audience:

- Which features can draw in new customers?
- Which ones might be less interesting or even scare off new customers?
- What should be my focus in case of paid marketing and advertising?

- Which existing users, images and advertising texts must shape my messages?

This evaluation can lead to impactful changes to your offer and generate new leads.

You should consistently revaluate your target audience. Carry out additional primary research every six months or annually and refine your consumer profile accordingly. As the market evolves, your ideal clientele must change with it. Stay ahead of the curve, so that you'll be one step forward from your competition.

Check Your Competition

Being a marketer, you can learn what strategies to stress on by observing your competitors. This will tell you which strategies are already efficient in your niche and how to evolve them into your marketing plans.

Use Existing Customer Data

Use the knowledge that you have already gained from existing customer data records when designing your marketing plan. Identify patterns in the data and utilize them smartly in your plan to develop a more impactful marketing strategy.

Use Google Analytics Data

Google Analytics is an excellent source for discovering patterns in your target audience. For example, the demographic information from Google tells information about the gender and age of your audience. This will enable you to understand your audience better and develop more relevant content for them, which will in turn generate more revenue for your business.

Recognizing the right audience is significant for your marketing campaigns. Unfortunately, not everyone will be interested in what you have to say or what you are selling, so you have to figure out the ones to focus on.

Target audience analysis enables you to create content for your customers which is more personalized according to their user personality. This will allow you to resolve and address your weaknesses and develop long-term relationships with your audience. It also promotes a high ROI and expands your business.

PREPARING AND DESIGNING YOUR WEBSITE

Website is your online brochure. Before building a website, consider what you want your website to do. Studying your competitors' websites will provide you a clear idea of what's best for you.

To create a website, follow seven basic steps.

Step 1: Register a Domain Name

The domain name should represent your products or services in order to make it easy for your customers to find your company through a search engine. They can also expect your domain name to be same as your company name.

Your email address also requires your domain name, since sending an email from a business address seems more professional even though you are free to use any email address.

Remember to renew your domain name before it expires or else your business can be vulnerable to cybercriminals.

Step 2: Find a Web Hosting Company

In order to get your domain name on the Internet, you require a web hosting company. Almost all Internet service providers provide web hosting services and will offer you multiple email addresses.

Monthly web hosting fees depend on the size of your website and the number of visits.

Step 3: Prepare the Content

Think and analyse about what you want your customers to be able to do through your website. This allows you to determine which sections or pages to be included. Think about what information or transactions your customers want and do so. Check if the website is structured so that they can more easily find and do what they need.

Just as you would hire a professional to design your website, you can also hire a professional to write and structure your content.

A well-designed, customer-friendly website only will help your business stand out from the crowd. With relevant and suitable content and images, customers can better understand your products and services and feel comfortable buying from your company.

Step 4: Build Your Website

You can either build your own business website or hire a professional web developer. Websites need to be kept up to date, so be sure to plan for ongoing maintenance.

You can always utilize a website publishing package to create your own website. These are similar to word processors but have built-in features to turn your text and images into web content and send them to your website.

You need to design your website so that it can be easily used on smartphones and other mobile devices. Optimizing your website for mobile means that the growing number of users accessing the Internet on phones and tablets can use your website on the go.

HELPFUL TIPS FOR BUILDING A WEBSITE

- Consider what your audience wants to know, not just what you want to tell them.
- Take professional help. An unprofessional website can put customers off.
- Update your site constantly, especially the price details.
- Check if your contact information is right and easy to find.

- Promote your website in your marketing collateral and include it on your business cards.
- Identify how to make your website easily discoverable by search engines like Google. This is known as SEO. A web developer can assist you with SEO for your website.

Step 5: Respect the Need for Speed

Keep your website running smoothly by keeping the software up to date, optimizing videos and images for faster downloads, and using a website server which can handle your bandwidth needs.

Step 6: Have a CTA

Every page on your business website must entice the reader to do something. In short, give them a CTA. The landing pages must encourage users to take a specific action, for example, call your company, buy a product, download a white paper, sign up for a service or do something else which benefits your business goals—the action: a button, a link or a clear word. If possible, keep it at the top of the page, so readers don't have to scroll down before they find the CTA.

Step 7: Keep Your Design Simple

Limit the use of fonts, colours and GIFs which can take your eyes off the focus of the web page. Short paragraphs and bullets also make information more verifiable and easier to read. I suggest limiting paragraphs to fewer than six lines.

If you follow the seven-step outline above, the website design process should go more smoothly. With a bit of research and planning, your website design will get more informed. If you follow a development and launch checklist, you won't miss any critical steps. And finally, maintaining a website protects the investments made in building the website. Ultimately, customers will be happier with your experience and see the value of your website.

EASY AND SECURE PAYMENT INTEGRATIONS

For customers to easily shop through your website or programme, having a convenient and secure payment gateway in your business is critical. A payment gateway is a safe technology which collects and transmits data from a customer to an acquirer and sends a notification to the customer of the acceptance or rejection of payment.

A payment gateway process involves verifying a customer's bank card details, ensuring the availability of funds, and allowing the merchant to receive the payment for a product or service provided.

This technology is like an interface between a retailer's website and its buyer. Another function of secure payment gateway is the encryption of the confidential data on the customer's credit card in order to enable the anonymous transmission of customer data to the acquirer. The payment gateway process acts as middleware between buyer and seller and provides secure payments. Using a secure online payment gateway greatly simplifies the required software delivery process for merchants.

As mentioned above, this technology also manages sensitive user information such as bank card number, expiration date and CVV code.

HOW IS THE PAYMENT GATEWAY SAFE AND SECURE?

Payment gateways need to ensure that merchants are always receiving funds from customers at the time of purchase and that they do not have to worry about credit risk and the possibility of fraud.

However, it is almost impossible to prevent fraud completely. Scammers are always improving their methods, and therefore any disaster can happen to anyone. But by using a secure payment gateway, you can significantly reduce the risk of fraud and prevent theft. Here are several ways you can provide secure payment on your website.

Secure Sockets Layer for Secure Connections

Secure Sockets Layer (SSL) must protect all transactions made through your company's website or mobile app. With the help of SSL, it is possible to encrypt the confidential data on your customers' bank cards and thus protect them from fraudsters.

The use of such technologies increases payment security and increases the customers' willingness to buy. A lock symbol indicates SLL in the address bar, and web addresses begin with https.

When a user sees an icon like this, they understand that they can shop safely through your website and do not have to worry about the security of their data.

The secure payment provider you use must ensure that they use https for all of their services and therefore have an SSL certificate.

You should also periodically review the information about the certification authorities you or they use. Again, this helps maintain a high level of payment security.

Payment Card Industry

Certified Payment Card Industry (PCI) is required when processing payments on your website. The PCI Data Security Standard (DSS) contains guidelines which merchants must strictly follow to safely protect sensitive user data when processing payments. Some of the requirements include the following:

- Use validated payment software at the POS or in the website's shopping cart.
- Do not store sensitive customer data on computers.
- Encrypt the transmission of customer data over an open public network.
- Use a firewall on networks and personal computers (PCs).
- Educate your employees about security measures, for example, the protection of cardholder data.

- One of the best news is that traders don't have to adhere to PCI standards. You just have to choose the best service provider.

Providers can have the payment gateway providers follow industry security standards and provide the data encryption required by PCI.

Therefore, the merchant can rely on a secure payment gateway if they adhere to these security standards. Hence, payment gateways act as third-party solutions which provide merchants with the latest and greatest security measures they need.

Tokenization

Tokenization replaces all sensitive user data with a randomly generated character set. Using this technology significantly reduces the risk of data loss. One of the finest methods is to use a token which is a real bank card number. After the transaction is over, the user's confidential data is sent to a special server where it is securely stored.

At the same time, the seller receives a unique number with which the customer can shop on the web or in the program. They do not have to enter all their data again; they can pay with one click.

The use of tokenized payment gateways helps to minimize the risk of payment fraud. You don't need to have all of your customer's data; save their bank and credit card details on your server. It is also essential that the data is encrypted before it reaches the database server.

3D Secure Authentication

3D Secure is basically a messaging protocol encompassing four domains: the bank, the technology, processing transaction, and the issuing bank.

This is an additional layer of security which prevents fraudulent transactions without a physical bank card. In addition, by using such technology, you automatically transfer responsibility for yourself to the issuing bank.

Suppose a user wants to shop on the Internet. In that case, they must therefore confirm the payment with a generated password or a unique PIN, which the bank sends via SMS, which contributes to a considerable increase in defence.

OPEN YOUR BUSINESS PAYMENT GATEWAY

After understanding the significance of any payment gateway and how it impacts your revenue and security, it is time to take the following steps:

- **Do your research with the main priorities:** Review your potential payment solution for PCI compliance to make sure it is secure, and always consider transaction prices to get an idea of how any gateway affects your bottom line.

- **Understand customers' wants:** Even if you lack a payment gateway, you may have the information needed. For example, which payment services are preferred by your customers, and how can these preferences be most conveniently supported?

- **Stack multiple gateways to fill in gaps:** There is no need to commit to a gateway for the rest of your days. You can stack numerous gateways at the same time for maximum coverage of customer needs.

With a better understanding of the gateway's functionality, price and security, your company can decide the right option for its business needs and include a new level of security (and peace of mind) which customers buy when conducting an online business.

You might not have bundles of money to spend on marketing in the early stages of your start-up, but there are other effective ways to get your brand out there.

ADVERTISING, PROMOTING AND MARKETING YOUR ONLINE BUSINESS

Before the arrival of the Internet, small businesses had very few ways to market their products cost effectively, such as by printing flyers or sponsoring small local events. But now there are so many options on the web; you just have to know where to look for.

Here are seven excellent ways of promoting your business online without spending a dime.

Use the Three Major Local Listing Services

Registering your business with Google Places makes it easy to search for Google and appear on Google Maps. You just have to fill the form and register and then verify your business through the verification process, which is done with a phone call or email. Yahoo! also has an extensive database of companies called Yahoo! Local. It's free, and it's definitely worth spending the few minutes to set it up. Microsoft's Bing has a very similar service which you can simply sign up for.

Use Social Media

Social media platforms are not just any tool to get known; now, they have become a mandatory time investment for all businesses. For example, you can link ads and offers on your Facebook group and have a direct channel to your customers on Twitter. Networking on LinkedIn, on both personal and business levels, is another way of expanding your start-up.

Start a Blog

Not only does an excellent blog help your online business get your name out there, but it also connects you more deeply with your consumers. However, remember that one of the most important keys to blogging is keeping your blogs active as often as possible. An inactive and abandoned blog is worthless.

Post Multimedia Content to YouTube and Flickr

YouTube is a free means to spread creative and promotional videos but, to be successful, you need to post content which the masses want to see, and that is also relevant to your business. A simple advertisement won't function. A Flickr profile provides you with a place to collect all of your business photos and link them to your site.

SEO of Your Site

SEO is not to be undermined in the world of constant search on Google. Search online for a book or handy guide on SEO and check if your website is prepared for search engine performance.

Press Releases

Feel free to publish a press release; maybe people will notice. They are a powerful media tool for promoting, and distributing them for free is a bonus.

Join and Contribute to Online Community

Every particular niche has some online communities to participate in. But logging into a forum and posting about your business every now and then will not do anyone any good and may disappoint people. Actively participate and build a relationship with the community even while keeping your online business away from it.

Passively promote your online business by including a link in your signature or only mentioning it only when the context is appropriate.

Remember that when you pay for advertising, you need to keep an eye on your ROI. Getting better visibility for your brand is great, but it might not be worth it if the advertising costs aren't bringing the company in revenue.

Think about your ideal audience and how they enjoy consuming media. If there is a specific need that you can satisfy and convey to potential customers, they will likely give it a try. But as with all aspects of running a successful business, be willing to be patient and keep trying new methods to promote your business successfully.

These seven strategies should give you some ideas on how to promote your business. Every marketing activity you undertake should increase your brand awareness with your target audience.

MANAGING YOUR ORDER FULFILMENT AND EVERYDAY BUSINESS OPERATIONS

Order processing represents the entire process of getting, packing and sending online orders to customers. You have the option of processing your orders internally or outsourcing them to an external logistics company (3PL) which offers storage, technology and employees for fulfilling orders flawlessly and fast.

When you start out, products are often delivered straight to the customer's home, or they rent storage space and then hire someone to help with the order. This strategy is doable the first time you're building a business, but it can soon hit order fulfilment if orders triple.

If you are doing everything right and your business continues to grow, your order fulfilment process must change.

Here are three main factors to consider affecting your overall compliance strategy, especially as your business grows.

Order Volume

If you send small orders, it is sufficient to send the packages yourself. But once you hit 200 orders or more per month, the self-fulfilment process becomes less effective, and you run out of time to concentrate on other fields of your business which need your attention.

Once you get high in volume, there's a lot more to keep account of, be it inventory, SKU speed or inventory replenishment, what is ongoing shipping, where the orders are being shipped to, and what items are to be returned.

Technology

Technology plays an important role in terms of order processing. It's not merely about having the correct number of people to get the task done but also about having the accurate data and information to handle everything.

By connecting the order fulfilment software to your virtual store, you can streamline the whole procedure. Some third-party logistics companies must be technology-driven, which implies that they are possessed with a range of technologies which automate and streamline the ordering process for more accurate order fulfilment.

Technology-driven third-party logistics provides the analysis and technology to enable you to predict the demand and analyse which of your warehouses to keep your inventory in, in order to reduce shipping costs.

Location

The place where your inventory is kept and orders are shipped can be a strategic differentiator for any online business. Location is vital, as it affects the distance and time taken by your packages by eliminating shipping to the highest and costliest zones.

An important advice is to store inventory in or near a major city or any central location so that you can reach a greater volume of customers. In addition, if you are working with any third-party logistics company which has multiple locations to store inventory, you can always expand your scope and reduce shipping costs and lead times.

HOW IS ORDER FULFILMENT ACCELERATED?

The easiest way to accelerate order fulfilment is to automate processes, leverage data and outsource order fulfilment.

Automation of Processes

There are many steps which don't have to be done manually but can be automated, including checking for any new orders. Leveraging technology such as inventory management software can prove to be fruitful in automating parts of the process, such as setting up inventory reorder points, creating picking lists and managing returns.

Outsourcing fulfilment to a technology-enabled third-party logistics is yet another way to automate fulfilment, with orders being automatically packed and shipped for you as soon as any order is placed and assigned to the fulfilment centre which has preserved the inventory and bring you closer to your end customer.

Using Data

Data is true power. You can make better business decisions by utilizing the data to create and enhance your overall order fulfilment strategy. For example, historical order data can provide insights into the upcoming order demand to avoid potential stock shortages. In addition, the use of technology provides real-time data so that you always know the amount of stock available and not rely on static snapshots of the past.

Fulfilling the Outsource

While self-fulfilment appears to be the most economical way to handle orders (while managing over the process), it can slow fulfilment time and increase shipping expenses in the long run.

Customers aspire of fast shipping, and there is absolutely no shortcut to delivery. While a few traders have successfully fulfilled their orders on their own, many have discovered that outsourcing the fulfilment was one of the best decisions they ever made.

CONVERTING BROWSERS INTO BUYERS

Attracting customers to your business is only the first part of the retailer's challenge. As soon as they are at the door, you still have to convince them to buy. So here's a simple approach that speaks to human nature and works: Get shoppers to touch and manipulate products.

Running Shopping Campaigns on Google AdWords

Shopping campaigns are greatly impactful and generally convert much better compared to the search campaigns. This is because customers can compare the prices right on the search page, so one click is more likely to convert. Plus, the audience can already view an image of the product, and images have always proved to be a great conversion driver.

In addition, you only need one feed to campaign on potentially all of the items in your e-commerce. This saves you a lot of set-up time and lets you to find potentially profitable items rapidly. Campaigns are also extremely easy to handle and maintain, making them an ideal marketing tool for online stores.

Remarketing through Shopping Traffic

As we have just discussed, shopping campaigns generate a lot of website traffic. You can utilize this traffic by remarketing all users who visited your website via a shopping campaign but did not convert. There are high chances that they might convert on a second visit because they are already familiar with your brand.

You just have to develop a personalized listing for your website visitors who have not yet converted.

Cautious Price Research

Your product pricing plan brings in a huge difference to the success of an e-commerce store. The more standardized a product is, the more price-sensitive consumers become before they buy it. Turn your weekly job into researching ongoing market prices for your most essential items. Don't trade outside of the market.

The key to turning browsers into buyers is to create a seamless and relevant path to purchase, removing barriers and inaccuracies. Most importantly, you have to aim to provide transparency and consistency in the customer journey.

SOME FINAL THOUGHTS ON E-COMMERCE

There are plenty of ways you can quickly grow your online store, and it just takes time, energy and money. There are no shortcuts, but the payouts can be worth it. The market opportunities are still tremendous, so do not despair. If you have a killer product and you are willing to put serious effort into your store, the possibilities are endless.

CHAPTER 16

MAKE MONEY VIA SELLING ON AMAZON

As the pandemic has extended from 2019 to 2021, we have also witnessed disruptive changes such as work from home, consumer preference towards online shopping, digital payments and adapting to the new normal during these extended times of survival. During the pandemic, the sales of the well-established e-commerce businesses surged. One of the promising platforms for these e-commerce entities was Fulfillment by Amazon (FBA).

Selling on Amazon India is one of the best ways to make money online. If you are equipped with the right strategies and approaches about what products to sell and know exactly how things work, selling on Amazon can be very profitable. If you want to set up a full-time business or generate a side income for your family, becoming a seller on Amazon is one of the best options for you.

In this chapter, let us explore how you can make money using the feature of FBA in India.

WHY SHOULD YOU SELL ON AMAZON?

Let's look at some of the statistics of Amazon India.

- Over 100 million users are registered on Amazon in India.
- Amazon is offering 168 million products to its Indian customers.
- 218,000 sellers actively sell on Amazon India and are growing.

- Amazon's revenue in India for FY 2020 was ₹11,028 crore, up from ₹7,777 crore in 2019.
- Amazon Prime in India has 10 million users.
- Amazon India is the largest online smartphone channel, with 47 per cent market share.
- With orders from over 99 per cent serviceable PIN codes in India, Amazon has become the online destination for small and medium-sized enterprises.[1]

Looking at these numbers, it is evident that an active customer base is readily available here. In addition, a wide range of products are sold, so your product is very much likely to fit in, unlike retail-only or grocery-only marketplaces. Alongside, if Amazon can store, pack and ship your products, that is, if Amazon fulfils your orders, doesn't this sound like a steal deal for you?

WHAT PRODUCT CATEGORIES CAN YOU SELL ON AMAZON?

As we have already seen, Amazon is selling millions of products to its customers. The broad categories of products that Amazon sells include baby products; beauty products; books; consumer electronics; digital accessories such as mobile accessories, electronic accessories and computer accessories; home improvement items, jewellery, kitchen essentials, luggage, mobile phones, movies, personal care appliances, PCs, tablets, toys, video games and watches. This list is dynamic, and Amazon keeps adding categories depending on customer demand! You can sell any product/s which will broadly fall into the categories sold by Amazon.

---

[1] https://sellercentral.amazon.in/gp/help/external/G200178470?language=en_IN (accessed on 25 July 2021).

Note: There are restrictions on selling specific products on Amazon such as weapons and animals. Please check the restricted product list on the Amazon India website.[2]

HOW TO START SELLING ON AMAZON?

Once you have finalized the product you want to sell on Amazon. in, your next step is to enrol as a seller on Amazon India. After getting the approval, you should list your product/s under the correct category.

After you successfully list your product, the next step is where you should decide how you would like to fulfil customer orders.

There are three options that you can choose as an Amazon seller:

Merchant Fulfilled: Here, you hold your inventory at your location, and you will be responsible for delivery to the customer whenever there is an order. So as a seller, you should arrange for all packaging and shipping. Amazon will notify the customer order to you on your email and also on its Seller Central dashboard. You need to pack and fulfil the order.

Amazon Easy Ship: It is a service where an Amazon delivery person will pick your package from your location and deliver it to the customer's doorstep whenever there is an order. If you choose Easy Ship, your customers can track their orders and delivery date and get the cash on delivery feature. The Easy Ship feature is suitable if you have your warehouse and you deal with a variety of products. However, under this option, you have to maintain inventory at your warehouse and pack as per Amazon's requirements.

Fulfillment by Amazon: If you opt for this, then Amazon will store your product at its warehouse. Then, when a customer orders your product, Amazon will pack and ship your product directly to the customer. However, Amazon will charge fees for providing these

---

[2] https://sell.amazon.in/sell-online/fulfillment-by-amazon.html#fba-fees (accessed on 25 July 2021).

Table 16.1: Features of Three Selling Methods on Amazon

Features	FBA (Fulfillment by Amazon)	Easy Ship	Merchant Fulfilled
Storage	Storage fees	Borne by seller	Borne by seller
Packaging	Pick and pack fees	Borne by seller	Borne by seller
Shipping	Shipping fee	Shipping fee	Borne by seller
COD (cash on delivery)	Yes	Yes	No
Prime badge	Yes	By invite only	Only for limited customers
Customer service	Managed by Amazon	Managed by Amazon (optional)	Managed by seller

Source: https://tinuiti.com/blog/amazon/sell-on-amazon/ (accessed on 1 February 2020)

services. FBA is suitable if you are a new seller or don't want to deal with the hassles of storing, packing and shipping.

Table 16.1 gives you a summary of the features of the three selling methods on Amazon.in.

WHAT IS FBA?

After understanding the distinct features and benefits of the various methods of selling on Amazon, let us now focus in detail on the services provided under FBA and explore how to make money using FBA.

FBA can be considered as a one-stop solution to sell your products to Amazon customers. When you use FBA, all you need to do is send your products to Amazon fulfilment centres.

Fulfilment centres are Amazon's warehouses where your products are stored, packed and shipped to your customers. When a customer places an order, it will take care of packing, shipping and delivering the product to the customer's doorstep.

The added benefit is that opting for FBA gives your products the Prime badge, which offers same-day or next-day delivery for eligible customers. Amazon will also handle returns and customer support queries for you.

FBA has many benefits, but it costs you more and reduces your margins on each product. Nevertheless, if your product qualifies with the Prime badge and has the Amazon tag fulfilled, it can attract more customers. This likely increase in the sales volume should offset the drop in the margins per unit sold.

HOW CAN FBA BENEFIT YOU?

If you are already a seller of a product or are planning to sell, then Amazon FBA can benefit you in the following ways.

- **No need to have your warehouse:** You can store your products in Amazon's warehouses (saves you from the effort of holding your inventory, warehouse space and labour).

- **Hassle-free inventory management:** Amazon will manage your inventory, for example, storing at the right place, displaying the quantity in stock and intimating when product is out of stock. Your job is to replenish the stock as and when the products get sold.

- **Effortless logistics:** When a customer orders your product, Amazon, a logistics giant, will pack, ship and deliver it to the customer's doorstep (relieves you from the hassles of packing and finding the exemplary delivery service for shipping to your customer).

- **Worry-free customer service and returns management:** Amazon also provides customer service and handles customer returns for your product.

- **Exceptional customer service:** Your products will also get the 'Prime badge', which means that your products will be eligible for same-day or next-day delivery for Prime customers.

- **Customer relationship opportunity:** Also, your product will carry the 'Fulfilled by Amazon' tag, which builds trust with your customers.

HOW DOES FBA WORK?

We are now aware of the benefits FBA offers to existing as well as new sellers. Let us look at the FBA process to get a deeper insight into its working. There are certain prior requirements to be completed before you can utilize the fulfilment feature. These are listed below.

Following are the initial set-up requirements:

- First, as a seller, you should request Amazon to enrol you as a seller in the FBA programme. You need to provide your company information, bank details and other details as per Amazon. in requirements.

- Amazon checks your company's background (with the details you have provided) and decides to fulfil the online seller requirements.

- Once you are accepted, you have to register the Amazon fulfilment centre as an additional place of business. This is required for tax purposes.

Then you can start listing your product/s and also specify the unit quantities.

Once you complete these initial set-up formalities, your selling process begins (refer to Figure 16.1).

1. You label the products and the packages (Amazon.in Seller Central will guide you on this) and ship them to the fulfilment centre.

2. Amazon will receive the packages and store them in the fulfilment centre.

3. The customer places an order for your product.

4. Amazon will directly ship it from its fulfilment centre.

5. If there is any customer service required, Amazon.in will handle it.

6. Product returns, if any, are also managed by Amazon.in.

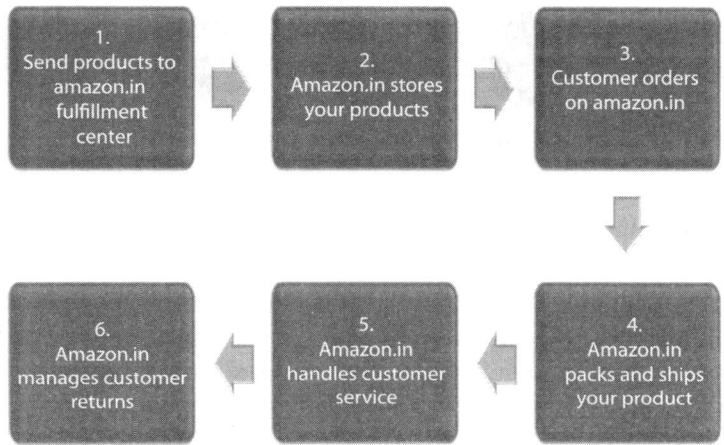

Figure 16.1: Diagrammatic Representation of the Amazon.in FBA Process Flow

WHAT ARE THE FEES FOR SELLING ON AMAZON USING FBA?

Well, by this time, you are knowledgeable about the various activities involved in the FBA process. It also reiterates how hassle-free your selling process can become by opting for FBA. However, Amazon.in charges you fees for providing all these services. Typically, Amazon charges four main fees in the FBA programme (refer to Figure 16.2). They are referral fee, closing fee, warehouse handling (shipping fee) and others (storage, pick and pack fee).[3]

The good news is that the FBA programme charges on a 'pay-as-you-go' basis only. It means that the storage charges will be only for the space occupied by your product (as per Amazon's guidelines) and handling, and shipping charges are charged only when there are customer orders.

---

[3] https://www.amazon.in/gp/help/customer/display.html?ref=hp_left_v4_sib?ie=UTF8&nodeId=G3UA5WC5S5UUKB5G (accessed on 26 July 2021).

Figure 16.2: Fees Charged by Amazon.in for FBA Services

Referral fee is charged as a percentage of sales and is fixed for each product category. The closing fee is fixed based on the price of the product. In addition, a fixed amount is charged towards storage, picking and packing. Shipping fee is charged based on the customer's location, and charges vary for local, regional and national limits. Applicable GST will be charged on all the fees.

Out of the payment received from the customer, Amazon will deduct the charges and transfer the balance amount directly to your bank account within five–seven business days.

HOW TO MAKE MONEY USING FBA?

Amazon.in claims that by switching to the FBA mode, its sellers have scaled their business up to 3×. Here are some guidelines and strategies to help you make money using FBA.

Choose the Right Product

- Choose a product which is likely to solve the problem of the customer. For example, categories such as organizers, electronics, kitchenware, health products, sporting equipment and accessories, and books are going to be helpful to customers.

- Look for customized products which are trendy and in-demand but are not readily available. Such categories will help in capturing the market and business growth.

- Sell the products you are passionate about such as sports equipment, electronic accessories, apparel, home decor or home improvement—whichever is close to your heart. You are likely to be more dedicated and inspired even during the challenging times of the business.

- A good vendor knows the target market and target purchasers quite well. Try to define your target customer and find out their needs. For example, high-fashion products attract adolescents and young ladies. Similarly, for baby products, your target customers are new parents or to-be parents.
- See how the market is performing and what the customers are searching for.
- Using the same link, you can also check out 'hot new releases' to explore bestselling new products. You can also find out what products are most wished for and which ones are the most gifted.
- Analyse and try to assess the gaps in these product parameters. Then you can consider giving extra or new valuable features in the product which can delight the buyers, for example, offering a colour variant in the product or pairing it up with another product, or attaching your brand name. It helps to build your image rapidly and increase sales too!
- A word of caution! Avoid selling products which may be eye-catching but do not have enough margin to cover the costs and make a profit.
- Do thorough product research and select those products which have high sales but with less competition. You can explore the Amazon bestsellers product page and hot selling new products page (as discussed earlier) for your product research.
- Brainstorm and list as many products as possible which are high in sales and low in competition.
- Spot those products which you can sell under a private label. Private-label products are manufactured or provided by one company and then labelled with another company's brand.
- The differentiation is significantly less with well-known brands. However, if you go with private label products, you can source at a reasonable cost and sell at a higher price by differentiating your offering. This is a sure way to enjoy high profits.

- Avoid products having seasonal demand, as it can affect your regular sales. For example, products like candles may be in high demand during Christmas. Festive decor sales may increase only during the festival season.

- Choose niche products; they will help you differentiate and stand out from your competitors. For example, selling 'oxidized jewellery' or 'hand-painted jewellery' would be easier to differentiate and sell at a better price than ordinary jewellery.

- Select those small and light products; this will benefit you in terms of storage and handling fee and shipping. So sell small and easy-to-pack products.

- Scout for the supplier or manufacturer of the product. You can check relevant Internet sites and negotiate a good deal with your suppliers. Keeping the costs low is the key to profits!

- Once you start making a profit on any one product and have a good number of customer reviews, keep adding to your product line! Think about the big picture; target adding to your basket of products. Think of creating your brand as that will pay off in the long run.

Analyse Competition

- Find out who your competitors are. Then list all those sellers who are selling the same product as yours.

- If your competitor is selling the same product and has thousands of reviews, it is more likely to buy from that competitor. Therefore, selling such a product will be very challenging for you.

- So, from your list, pick those products which do not have too many reviews. This way, you can make sure you have the right product, where competition is neither too much nor too little.

- You can also check on other sites like Google Trends to analyse if your shortlisted product is in demand.

- Compare prices offered by your competitors for your product on Amazon. See if you can charge a higher price point by making your product unique or offering some differentiation.
- Avoid getting into a 'price war' with your competitors by lowering the product prices.
- You can keep your competition low by selling at higher price points, but you should also deliver the right value to your customer.
- Price your product keeping in mind your cost price plus all other costs: shipping, warehousing, marketing and promotional expenses. Then, depending on the product volume and your expected sales, you can include a healthy profit margin to arrive at the product price (refer to Exhibit 16.1).

Exhibit 16.1. Calculation of Fees

Let's take an example: You are selling product 'A' whose price is ₹300.

Say the referral fee as per the product category is 4 per cent, that is, ₹12.

The closing fee as per the category is ₹12.

For a standard size item, the storage is ₹20, the pick and pack fee is ₹10 and the shipping fee is around `25 (it depends on whether the shipment is local, regional or national).

So your total fee is ₹79 (₹12 + ₹12 + ₹20 + ₹10 + ₹25).

Add applicable GST, say @ 18 per cent, that is, ₹14.22.

So your total fee including GST is ₹93.

Let's say you bought product 'A' originally at ₹150.

Then the total cost is product cost + total fee + GST = ₹150 + ₹79 + ₹14 = ₹243.

If you sell product 'A' at ₹300, then you make a profit of ₹57 (₹300 − ₹243) or 23.5 per cent.

Note: This is a conservative estimate; you can have higher margins if you can procure from low-cost sources and/or you offer differentiated quality products.

The example given is for educational purposes only. Refer to Amazon.in for actual calculations.

Manage Customer Reviews

- Customer reviews are precious and are significant optimization factors which will lead to more sales. These also help to rank your product higher.

- If your product has a high number of positive reviews, the conversion rate also grows dramatically.

- First and foremost, make sure your product is excellent before moving on to the reviews. You must sell an excellent product if you want a positive review!

- Amazon allows customers to write a product review and give a star rating. Additionally, images or videos can also be added to the review.

- As you are aware, reviews help customers in deciding whether to buy a product or not. Hence, reviews for your product should be authentic feedback. Amazon has a 'zero-tolerance' policy for reviews which are intended to deceive and manipulate customers.

- Read all the policies and be familiar with the right way to get more product reviews and avoid policy violations. For example, if you get a review in exchange for a monetary reward or get a review from your family circles, Amazon will not allow and remove the review.

- The list of unacceptable reviews is available on Amazon.in website.[4] Make sure your customer reviews don't fall under any of the policy violations.

- Here are five proven ways to get authentic product reviews:

    o Within 5–30 days of purchase, you can use Amazon's 'Request a Review' button which allows you to manually request reviews for each of your orders in Seller Central. Amazon will send an email to the customer on your behalf

---

[4] https://www.amazon.in/gp/help/customer/display.html/ref=hp_left_v4_sib?ie=UTF8&nodeId=G3UA5WC5S5UUKB5G (accessed on 26 July 2021).

to obtain a product review and seller rating when you use this.

- Amazon discourages you from asking your customers through email or buyer–seller messaging.

    o You can use product inserts. Along with your product, you can thank the customer to leave feedback on the Amazon website. You can also provide your social media links here. You can request the customer to reach out to you if there are any issues with the product or the service. However, make sure your insert does not violate Amazon's policies, for example, incentivizing positive reviews.

    o You can avail social media opportunity, In your social media campaigns, you can request the customers to leave honest feedback. As social media has the potential to increase your sales, so will be the chances to increase your reviews! But, again, a word of caution: Don't campaign for the positive feedback. Always request an honest review.

    o You can use third-party automated review request services. You can also utilize the services of a third party who specializes in automated review request systems. In addition to Amazon's review request, the third-party system uses the Amazon platform to manage your reviews.

You can use Amazon SPN India. The Service Provider Network (SPN) provides varied requirements on the Amazon network in one solution. It is a third-party paid service but approved by Amazon. The services include imaging, cataloguing, shipping, review and return management, to name a few.

Promote Your Products

As you are aware, there can be thousands of sellers on Amazon.in for each product category. So it isn't easy to appear on the first page of search results with only organic reach. Therefore, it is wise to have a promotional budget for your product and run sponsored ads on Amazon. When you run ads, your product appears on the top of the search pages. This helps to gain visibility among customers and, in turn, increases your sales. Successful sellers have increased their sales volumes by 40 per cent with very low advertising spend, using Amazon Sponsored Products.[5]

However, before running ads, you need to have the following in place:

- Your product should be of good quality and useful to the customer. (Any number of ads cannot induce high sales if your product quality is inferior!)
- Use SEO techniques in your product listing by using keywords at the right places.
- Always use high-quality, professional-looking images. Images capture customers' attention and speak about the quality of the product.

Now you are ready to promote your product on Amazon by running your ad. There are four ways in which you can run ads. Let us explore each one in detail.[6]

1. **Sponsored Products:** Sponsored Products are ads for individual product listings on Amazon.in. These appear on product detail pages and shopping results pages. These can help you target customers who are ready to buy and are actively searching for the products they require.

    - Whenever a customer searches for the keywords of your product, Amazon will display your product ad alongside the search results. You have to bid for these ads. You only pay when the customer clicks on the ad.

2. **Sponsored Brands:** Your brand and product portfolio are displayed in Sponsored Brands. Your business logo, a personalized

---
[5] https://sell.amazon.in/grow-your-business/advertise (accessed on 18 February 2022).
[6] https://sell.amazon.in/grow-your-business/advertise.html (accessed on 26 July 2021).

headline and a selection of your products are all shown in these ads. In addition, they are displayed on shopping results pages to increase product visibility and sales. Sponsored Brands allow you to easily draw attention to your brand and products among buyers looking for similar items.

3. **Amazon Store:** Amazon Store is a free self-service feature where sellers with a registered brand can generate content which inspires, educates and helps customers discover your brand's product assortment. It is a merchandising and advertising tool which allows sellers to set up a multi-page website for their products. Here, you have many customizable features to showcase your product uniquely, such as image, video and text.

4. **Headline Search Ads (PPC):** This works similarly to the Sponsored Product except that Headline Search Ads are placed prominently above search results on Amazon. This placement is very attractive and can help you get more traffic.

Other than these, you can also use the power of social media to gain visibility. It is seen that, on average, Indians spend 2.25 hours every day on social media. You can display your product listings or your promo codes on your social media sites such as Instagram and Facebook and share the Amazon link to buy your product. However, all your promotions should be within the guidelines provided by Amazon.in.

With the right product strategy, a thorough competitor analysis, competitive pricing, honest customer ratings, authentic customer reviews and cost-effective product promotion, it is a killer strategy for skyrocketing sales and encashing profits!

Once you follow these guidelines and strategies, you will see an increase in your customer orders. As FBA is professionally fulfilling your order, you can sit back and enjoy the profits. Now that you are well-equipped with all the tips and tricks, you can certainly make money using FBA.

CHALLENGES OF SELLING ON AMAZON

Like any business, selling on Amazon is not void of challenges. Here, let's discuss some of the significant challenges Amazon sellers face and look at probable solutions.

1. **Intense competition:** Online selling on Amazon gives you access to customers spread all over the county. Great! Similarly, it also consists of sellers from all over India. Fair enough! Therefore, your competitors are also more on the online space. One of the ways to solve this is to enter the high-price segment where there is relatively less number of sellers than to compete in the low-price segment where the competition is more and margins are also significantly less.

2. **Price war among competitors:** Due to intense competition, sellers resort to compete on the price and decrease the prices, hoping to achieve more sales. However, this only is an end game, as it reduces the margins for all the sellers, and hence nobody benefits. To solve this, as a seller, try not to enter into a price war. Instead, try to customize and differentiate your offering. Provide better-quality products which add value to customers. Acquire good customer reviews.

3. **Changes or suspension of your Amazon seller account:** If Amazon thinks that you have violated any of its policies, then the privileges in your seller account may be withdrawn, or Amazon may suspend your account. Please read and understand the policies and try to follow the same. Obtaining fake customer reviews and the likes should be avoided.

4. **Uncertainty of sales:** Your current product sales do not assure that the same trend will continue in the coming months. This can lead to a decrease in your product sales over some time. Please do not depend on a single product to perform, as every product has its life cycle. Instead, please keep your eyes and ears open for the new trends which are setting in, research about them and keep adding them into your sales basket!

5. **Complexities in product ranking on Amazon search:** Amazon keeps changing its algorithms for its product ranking. These changes can mean that your product ranking falls considerably if you do not keep pace with that. Consider hiring an expert or updating yourself on the changing SEO aspects, insert high-quality images and use keywords at the right places in your description for organic growth. Also, run sponsored ads to gain better visibility. With the proper perspective and long-term business goal, working around the challenges and staying put in the business are possible.

Amazon.in, as a marketplace, is expanding and adding new products depending on its customer needs. Now, due to the COVID-19 pandemic, more customers have turned to online shopping. Considering this as an opportunity and being equipped with the right strategies and thorough research, you can make money using Amazon FBA. The tips and strategies discussed in this chapter are aimed to give you some pointers on your journey to start selling on Amazon.

CHAPTER 17

MAKE MONEY WITH DROPSHIPPING

What product will you sell to your customer? How will you source its supply? How can it be delivered quickly? There are many ways of sourcing the products. You can manufacture the products and sell to buyers, but that's a very long process, is time-consuming and can lead to financial challenges.

In starting an online business, the key element is the product. As an alternative, you can buy from a manufacturer in bulk and then deliver the products to the buyers.

This process is a bit risky and expensive because one must invest money in buying stock and need a store to keep the inventory safely, and there is a chance of incurring losses if enough sales are not there.

As we all know, every problem has a solution, so here's a way to conduct a business online without manufacturing products and buying and storing inventory. The process is called dropshipping. It is an easy, fast and low-risk way to get started with online business.

However, one should know all the nuances to succeed in dropshipping.

WHAT IS DROPSHIPPING?

Dropshipping is a type of e-commerce business model. However, it is different from other e-commerce platforms, as it is a way of selling without carrying any inventory or stocks.

Usually, if a business wants to sell its product using an e-commerce platform, it would need to hold inventory or stocks. And this could now incur a business expense upfront. Having own products may give higher profit margin but there will always be a barrier in terms of cost. But in dropshipping, there is no need to hold any inventory or stock. You just need to build your e-commerce store, and after creating it, you have to put up the product's images and give a short description about it. And then, if any customer reaches out to your e-commerce store and selects the product and wants to purchase it, then you will be selling them, but the shipment of the products will not be your responsibility. There's a supplier you are dealing with regarding the products, and that supplier will take up the responsibility of shipment of products. After getting the customer order, you just need to give full details of the customer to the supplier you were working with and make sure that your supplier ships out that particular product to a specific address.

In this whole process, the owner of the e-commerce, e-store or dropshipper just acts as the middleman between the supplier and the customer and helps both of them in satisfying their needs and wants.

The significant difference between the dropshipper and the supplier is that the dropshipper doesn't hold the stocks or inventory. However, the supplier has to keep the stocks, and if the stock gets over, the supplier has to purchase it from a third party, the wholesaler or manufacturer, to fulfil orders.

In the end, once the product is shipped, the dropshipper receives the payment, and then they transfer the amount of the product to the shipper and keep the remaining amount as their profit.

HOW DOES DROPSHIPPING BUSINESS MODEL WORK?

Dropshipping starts with making a website and then listing product images on your website. After listing the products, the website requires traffic to initiate the buying process, and to drive the traffic, websites need to put content regularly, such as posting blogs, posting on social media and email marketing. Websites can also run Facebook and

Instagram ads. All this strategy will help engage with the audience, which leads to more traffic to the website. The audience always wants to get educated, and by doing all these, you are educating them about the products and telling them how these products can enhance their lives by using marketing and selling skills.

If any customer purchases through your website, you need to connect with the supplier you are working with, who will ship out the product to the customers. In this way, the customer gets its product without even knowing that you were only a dropshipper.

Let us now understand the benefits of dropshipping business model.

BENEFITS OF DROPSHIPPING

Many people consider dropshipping to start with, because in a short time, you can learn about the market and can test many different ideas. Some other benefits of dropshipping are as follows.

- **Less capital required:** Requirement of capital is significantly less in this business, allowing anyone to start without any financial constraint. Initially, you just need to invest in a domain and hosting, which barely has any cost, and then invest in ads.

- **Easy to start:** Starting a dropshipping business is much easier than running a retail business. A dropshipper never worries about managing any warehouse, packing or shipping of goods, or any kind of handling returns and inbound shipments.

- **Flexibility of places:** A dropshipping business can be started from anywhere in the world, whether you are in a smaller country or a big country. You just need a good Internet connection and resources to get in touch with the suppliers and customers. Suppose that if you are located in a country where people don't buy; you don't need to move to other countries. Instead, you can quickly start in a country where people buy more.

- **Massive potential growth:** Dropshipping is not a one-night game which will make anyone rich overnight. Although it has enormous potential, it just requires more patience and the right processes to succeed. There are many dropshippers out there who are making a very handsome amount. You just need to pick the right niche.

- **Low risk involved:** Risk Involvement is relatively low, as you are not handling any inventory and not investing on a large scale, so there is no chance of losses. If you spend more budget on ads and marketing, cost will still be low as compared to traditional retail business.

DISADVANTAGES OF DROPSHIPPING

There is not a single business which does not have any disadvantages. In every industry, there is competition and barriers which come in the way, and dropshipping has too.

- **High competition:** Many suppliers are working with many dropshippers, most of whom sell at the same price. Hence, there is no differentiation.

- **Low profit margin:** Profit margin is relatively low because of high competition. Compared to the online retail business, the margin is insufficient because you make only commissions from the product. Initially, it is tough to generate revenues. However, the more patience and time you will give, the more you will earn out of it.

- **Inventory problems:** A dropshipper never keeps an inventory; suppliers track which item is in and out of stock. If suppliers do not keep stock, then it's a problem for the dropshippers, as customers may place order which cannot be fulfilled.

- **No control over delivery:** The product delivery is the responsibility of the suppliers. There's no role of dropshippers in that. If suppliers make any error like not delivering the product on time or the wrong product gets delivered, this may cause a problem for your business because the customer makes their purchase from your e-commerce store.

Let us see the process you can follow to get started with dropshipping.

GETTING STARTED WITH DROPSHIPPING
Adding Value

Value is the most desirable thing all customers look for. To make a strong presence on a customer's minds, you need to do something more than your competitors.

Always make sure that you add more value to your products.

There are various ways by which you can add value to products.

- **Quality of products:** Quality is the power of a product. Best-quality products satisfy customers. Customers don't think of money if the product quality is up to the mark. But after paying, if the quality of the products is not up to satisfaction, you will lose the customer. They will be dissatisfied and disappointed. So always prefer to offer high-quality products to your customers.

- **Fast delivery:** Customers are impatient. They can't wait for so long. They want their order to get delivered the very next day after making a purchase. So customer fulfilment is a must, that is, good product quality with fast delivery.

- **Good packaging and design:** Presentation also has an impact on the product. Packaging can create an instant impression towards your business, which is a plus point.

- **Discount on products:** Discounts help in grabbing customer attention. Give offers and sales especially during festive season to lure the customers.

- **Branding:** People trust the brand; they recognize the product more as a brand. So make sure you create brand awareness which will generate interest and some people will buy.

The Correct Niche

Niche is a crucial factor in dropshipping. More dropshipping businesses fail because of choosing the wrong niche. Initially, one should never jump into a niche where competition is high.

Always prefer a low competition niche to make a successful entry in the dropshipping world.

Competitive Research

After selecting a niche, proper research and analysis are required in dropshipping to know more about the competitors. The competitive examination will help you understand the business landscape, tactics and strategies used by competitors. Also, this will help you in building a solid marketing strategy for your dropshipping business.

Marketing of E-commerce Store

You need to strategize such that your audience should feel that you are providing a solution to their problems. Offer a kind of service which will differentiate you from your competitors. Do what no one is doing.

Marketing can be done through various methods such as social media, email marketing and running ads on Google and Facebook.

Analysis of Offering

After doing proper marketing, wait for the response of your target audiences and see whether they are satisfied with the offers and services or demanding something more out of it. Then, as per the results, make your analysis, make changes and deliver the correct output that the audience demands.

IS DROPSHIPPING A LEGAL BUSINESS?

Considering anything as illegal without knowing or gaining knowledge about it is entirely wrong. Many people don't believe in such type of online business. So it is necessary to know facts about it before judging. Many do think that dropshipping is not legal or it's not 100 per cent genuine. But the matter of fact is that this is a wrong notion which stops them from starting a business.

Dropshipping is 100 per cent legal and 100 per cent genuine, though it has some legal aspects which you should follow.

The legal aspects are a business structure. Before starting dropshipping for your business, choose the proper business structure according to stability, future plans and preference. There are different kinds of business structures which can be considered before starting dropshipping.

Sole Proprietorship

A sole proprietorship is very simple and very easy to start. You will be your boss. All profits will be yours and you do not need to share with anyone. But you also must suffer from the losses alone, if any. If you get sued by anyone, there's a chance of losing your assets due to lack of liability protection.

Partnership Business

The partnership is done with two or more people which involves building a relationship between the partners. There is excellent support in a partnership business, but many dropshippers are sole entrepreneurs. In partnerships, profits and losses will be shared between the partners in the proportion of the partnership.

Limited Liability Company

Limit liability companies provide a separate legal entity, which means that dropshippers' business and personal finances are separated. Due to limited liability, this structure is preferred. Hence, if your dropshipping business grows, you can switch from sole proprietorship to a limited liability.

CHOOSING A DROPSHIPPING NICHE

Niche is an essential factor in online business. The whole success and failure of online business entirely depends upon choosing a correct and profitable niche. But, unfortunately, most entrepreneurs face difficulties and much confusion while deciding on the niche.

In the same way, the difficulties are also there in dropshipping. A niche with low competition and highest demand is considered the best niche for dropshipping. Niches which are long-standing are preferred. Also, if the niche has high demand, you may worry about intense competition it has.

Questions arise in mind about how to evaluate the ideas. Do follow the following guidelines for choosing your profitable niche.

Passion Consideration

Passion is all about interest which only comes for few things. No one can be passionate about everything. Everyone has their love in which they are the best among others—always consider your passion in choosing a niche. Never go with the thing that you are not passionate about. Always focus on the passion which will help you make the stairs of success despite all the challenges that come on the way.

Using Professional Experience

Having professional experience is an advantage in choosing a niche because you know the market and have the skill and knowledge about the niche. In addition, professionalism will lead you one step closer to your niche. And you will be able to provide the best service to your target audience.

Comparison of Demand for Products

After the awareness stage, the audience moves into the consideration stage, where they compare products and decide on the best products to buy, so the point is that when you jump to one niche for your dropshipping business, there are alternative products. Find the sales volume of the different products in the niche you are interested in. This will help you in getting a clear picture of the product which audiences are willing to buy. You can analyse the search volume by using some keyword tools.

CHOOSING A DROPSHIPPING PRODUCT

After choosing the niche, you must choose products within the niche. For example, a niche can be digital marketing and the product may be digital marketing course, affiliate marketing course or lead generation course.

In dropshipping, you can do business with various products. Moreover, one can change the products as per the market demand and competition. And this is an excellent benefit of dropshipping that you can change the products according to market trends.

Many dropshippers hop from one product to another in the hope of finding good results. If you want to earn money as fast as possible, you must keep adapting to the market trends.

Many strategies are there that you can consider while choosing a product.

Focus on Popularity

Choose products which have become more popular with time. Popular products have high competition in the market, but this is a plus point in dropshipping because it shows a chance of earning a good amount by selling that product. The more the competition is, the more is the money that can be made. So never be afraid of high competition. Initially, it will be challenging to enter a market, but making a decent income would be easy once you get started.

Endeavour to Go with the Niche

Underestimating the potential market for a product that is untapped could make you regret the decision. For example, suppose cats and dogs are trending animals, and the audience does get attracted towards them and buy them, but it doesn't mean that birds don't get sold in the market. It's just that its comparatively low, but the profit could be a bit higher.

Choose an Evergreen Niche

Evergreen products are all-time products in the market throughout the year. This kind of products have always been in demand because of everlasting appeal. Therefore, it will be an excellent strategy for beginners to step in dropshipping with evergreen products rather than seasonal products.

CHOOSING A SALES PLATFORM

After choosing the profitable niche and profitable products, the next step is selling. Where can these products be sold? Which platform is the best platform to sell?

There are multiple sales platforms where you can do dropshipping business. Every platform is different from the other. So it's essential to evaluate the review discussion on different forums and then make a wise decision. You can determine these platforms by using them also. Meaning that you can use all these platforms and then make an informed decision about which platform is working best for you.

Amazon

It is the world's largest e-commerce platform where almost all products are available. Amazon is one of the best dropshipping platforms which is famous worldwide, and because of popularity, there is no need to spend much on advertising the store. With a wide range of products available on Amazon, a lot of audiences enter this platform and trust the marketplace. And because of this enormous audience, the beginners may quickly get access to audience for their products.

But the questions that now arise are: How does dropshipping work on Amazon? Is it even profitable or not? And does it even cost any amount to start dropshipping on Amazon?

You can find answers to your questions here.

IS DROPSHIPPING ALLOWED ON AMAZON?

Yes, dropshipping is possible on Amazon. It allows the dropshipper to start their own business. Do follow all the terms and conditions of your seller agreement and policies of Amazon.[1]

HOW MUCH DOES IT COST TO START DROPSHIPPING ON AMAZON?

There is no cost to dropship on Amazon. But the fees of Amazon dropshipping products may vary by the type of product. It is usually in the range of 10–15 per cent. And if you are dealing with a relatively small dropshipping margin, it will take away a large portion of your profits.

Make sure that you choose a suitable selling plan. The individual plan will cost up to $0.99 per unit sold, and the professional plan will cost up to $33.99 per month, no matter how much sales you make.[2]

IS AMAZON DROPSHIPPING PROFITABLE?

Amazon dropshipping is and can be profitable. The average dropshipping margin is between 10 per cent and 30 per cent. Amazon takes around 15 per cent of the total revenue that you make.

Suppose if you are making a revenue of around 30 per cent, then Amazon will take 15 per cent of it, which mean your margin will be 15 per cent after selling a product on Amazon.

PROS AND CONS OF DROPSHIPPING ON AMAZON

Let us examine benefits and disadvantages of dropshipping on Amazon.

---

[1] https://sellercentral.amazon.com/gp/help/external/1791?language=en-US&ref=efph_1791_cont_201808410 (accessed on 7 December 2021).

[2] https://sell.amazon.com/pricing?ref_=asus_soa_rd& (accessed on 7 December 2021).

Pros

Trust and popularity: Amazon has a vast customer base. In addition, it is an established brand that everyone knows across the world. That's why you do not need to advertise about your store.

A trustworthy marketplace: With many customers and widespread business networks, Amazon has now become a trustworthy platform where customers are loyal as they buy repeatedly.

Variety of products: This is the best advantage as a dropshipper that anyone can have, because a product is very important and Amazon fulfils this requirement very easily.

Cons

Low profit margin: For a beginner, it is challenging to bear the selling fee (10%–15%), which is high on every item. This is really heartbreaking for the new dropshippers.

Difficulty in return policy: In traditional dropshipping, the returns of the product are handled by the manufacturers who take full responsibility, but in Amazon dropshipping, the retailers take over the responsibility of returned orders.

Upfront investment: To start dropshipping on Amazon, you need to arrange the products from supplier to meet Amazon requirements, which means that you need to make an upfront investment to start dropshipping on Amazon.

Let us now examine the process of dropshipping on Amazon.

START DROPSHIPPING ON AMAZON IN FIVE EASY STEPS

Choose an e-commerce platform: Shopify is the best option through which you can sell now on the world's largest marketplace, thanks to the partnership between Amazon and Shopify. This is the process through which you can now track and place orders by using the Amazon sales channel. You can do the following:

- Create a new product listing on Amazon.
- Give offers on existing products on Amazon.
- Link your Amazon product listing to your Shopify admin.

Create an Amazon seller account: If you need your product to get sold on Amazon, you have to create an Amazon seller account by heading over to sellercentral.amazon.com. There you have to give some essential details, for example, address, tax information and any other necessary information.[3]

Approval in category product: A seller is required to get approval on products which categorize in fashion, grocery, music, jewellery, watches, video and DVD, etc. These are all popular products which need to be approved before setting up an Amazon e-store.[4]

Link an Amazon account to Shopify: After creating an Amazon account, once it gets approved, make sure you connect your Amazon store to Shopify.

Create an Amazon product listing: Dropshipping on Amazon requires a product listing once you add a sales channel. This isn't going to happen automatically.

GlowRoad

GlowRoad is also a dropshipping platform and an app in India which provides an opportunity to millions of people, including students, homemakers and those who are unemployed, to start their own online business.

---

[3] https://sellercentral.amazon.com/ (accessed on 7 December 2021).

[4] https://sellercentral.amazon.com/gp/help/external/G200332540?language=en-US&ref=efph_G200332540_cont_200333160 (accessed on 7 December 2021).

All you need to do is create an account on the GlowRoad platform, select the product according to your niche that you want to sell and then search out for a great supplier who can make your work smoother and easier.

Once the supplier accepts your request, start advertising your products through paid ads via different social media platforms such as Facebook and Instagram.

Oberlo

Oberlo is another Indian dropshipping platform, and it's considered one of the best dropshipping platforms in India. So the beginners who are starting out fresh should go with this platform.

Be sure that you choose only high-demand and low-competition products. For example, in Oberlo, the product can easily be sourced from AliExpress to sell.

Wish

Wish is an essential sales platform with more than 250k daily active users and from more than nearly 80 different countries around the world. The audience spends more than half an hour shopping every day. So here is an excellent opportunity to start with a dropshipping business.

FINDING A DROPSHIPPING SUPPLIER

After deciding what and where, now is the time to search for the product sourcing, the source you can easily trust with all the process. You need to a find genuine and responsible supplier to ensure smooth business.

Selecting a good supplier is very critical and entails risk. Because in the end, whole dropshipping is dependent upon the supplier. They are the ones who ship out the product to the customer. So if you don't select the best supplier for your dropshipping business who are not punctual and are not best at their work, it would cause you many problems that you have to bear with later on.

So keep certain things in mind before selecting the suppliers.

What Makes a Supplier Good?

It is complicated for the ones who are just starting the dropshipping business. So it's imperative to check out some valuable points before selecting the suppliers.

- A supplier should provide fast shipping of products to the customer, because fast shipping makes the customer happier and increases engagement. Customers are highly impatient. They want their order to get delivered by the very next day at their doorstep.

- Make sure suppliers provide a high-quality and value-added product at a relatively low price. Customers always desire to have a high-quality product for themselves, no matter how much it costs because they see the high-quality products as a long-time investment, which makes them very satisfied and happy.

- Do check the staff of your supplier for whether they have a good, experienced team of staff members or not because great supporting team members can give the customer excellent service.

How to Find the Supplier?

The correct strategy helps in finding the right supplier with all the benefits. Here are the best methods that will work effectively.

- Contacting the manufacturer is the best way to find a supplier for the product you are interested in. Manufacturers of the products have a great understanding of the best supplier, and they can easily guide you to select the best supplier for your business. Also, they can save you from fake suppliers who are present in the markets as a supplier.

- A search engine is also a good option for searching out the supplier. The search engine can quickly locate the places of different suppliers of products. Make sure that after finding the supplier, you do a thorough investigation.

- Attending trade fairs is a good way to connect with other companies and suppliers. Moreover, it also helps get knowledge about advertising, marketing, product selection, etc.

- Placing an order from competitors who are also doing a dropshipping business can help get details of the supplier after receiving a package.

SETTING UP AN OWN ONLINE STORE

Setting up your online store means developing your website where you need to do many more things to rank your website on search engine pages. Your website will become your brand, making you stand out against your competitors. It's a plus point to have your own website because you will be the owner of your brand. The audience will call you a brand. And this is only possible when you follow the following steps.

Step 1: Getting a Domain Name

The very first and essential step in setting up an online store is getting a domain name. Choose a domain name that will represent your business. And make sure it is easy to pronounce and easy to remember for the audience, and it should relate to the products that you want to sell.

Don't go with a domain name which is hard to spell because the audience will end up looking for something else.

Step 2: Add Products to Your Online Store

After getting a domain and building a website, you can add various products to your online store without even holding any inventory because dropshipping is the only e-commerce business which allows running an e-commerce store without any stock.

Step 3: Add High-quality Product Images

Make sure you add high-quality product images on your product pages with all details and write convincing copies for your product with complete information. Also, you can give your customers discount, offer and flash sales on your product with a given time limit so that the audience will show interest in your product and make purchases.

Step 4: Set Up Payment Gateways

Payment gateways are essential in an online e-commerce store. Because, after all, audiences are making a purchase digitally, so they will also pay digitally, and it's necessary to provide an online payment system on your website. Make sure you put a payment gateway which works well like when a customer makes a purchase and is paying the amount of product, it must deduct the correct amount from the customer's bank account and make sure you receive the amount.

Many payment gateways are available which work well, for example, PayPal, Instamojo, Razorpay and Stripe.

Step 5: Start Marketing

After doing all the initial stages, now it's time to focus on marketing because if the audience doesn't come on the website, there will be no point in doing all the above.

There are multiple ways to drive traffic to your website. Some are free and some are paid. You can bring traffic organically through blogs and SEO on the website, which is free, and you can run paid ads.

ABOUT THE AUTHOR

Seema Gupta is a former professor of marketing at Indian Institute of Management (IIM) Bangalore. She is also a corporate trainer, consultant and speaker.

She is the author of the popular textbook *Digital Marketing*. Her book is used by many top B-schools in India. She has also authored the book *How People Buy Online*, published by SAGE.

She has published papers in reputed international journals such as *Information Systems Research* and *Journal of Marketing Theory and Practice*. She has presented papers in conferences across the world. She is the winner of the prestigious EFMD Best Global Case Writing Award and ISB-IVEY Best Case Award.

Prior to IIM Bangalore, she worked with Mudra Institute of Communications, Ahmedabad, and RPG Group.

She is a thought leader and democratizes knowledge in digital marketing by sharing it on her social media handles: www.Profseema.com, Instagram, LinkedIn and YouTube.

She is often quoted for her views on marketing issues in leading newspapers such as the *Times of India*, *Brand Equity*, *Financial Express*, *Rajasthan Patrika* and *Punjab Kesari*.

STAY ENCOURAGED • STAY CREATIVE • STAY MOTIVATED

Keep abreast of the most cutting-edge thinking driving businesses today.

For special offers on these books and more visit **steladeal.sagepub.in**
YOUR ONE-STOP-SHOP FOR LOWEST PRICE

www.sagepub.in